WALKS ON THE
WEST PENNINE MOORS

*Front Cover: Rivington Pike
across Lower Rivington Reservoir.*

Back Cover: Yarnsdale, above Entwistle Reservoir.

*Upper Rivington Reservoir with
Rivington Pike behind*

WALKS ON THE
WEST PENNINE MOORS

A COMPANION GUIDE TO THE
RECREATION AREA

by GLADYS SELLERS

Illustrations by R.B. Evans

CICERONE PRESS
MILNTHORPE, CUMBRIA

©Gladys Sellers 1979, 1987
First published 1979
Reprinted (revised) 1983
Second Edition 1988
ISBN 0 902363 92 1

ACKNOWLEDGEMENTS

I should like to thank the following friends for placing their local knowledge at my disposal: Miss A. Palmer, Mr. & Mrs. J. W. Rostron, the late Mr. W. Sherbourne, and the late Mr. P. L. Walkden. In addition I should like to thank Mr. T. Waghorn and Mrs. C. Bolton for updating me on developments at Holcombe. The responsibility for the selection and description of the walks, is, however, mine alone. I have drawn upon the various pamphlets produced on behalf of the West Pennine Moors Management Committee and other bodies for some of the background information in this book.

In addition I should like to thank Mr. J. Heyes, Deputy Librarian of the Chorley and District Library for his assistance with my searches for information.

Gladys Sellers, 1987

CONTENTS

A NOTE ABOUT THE AUTHOR

Gladys Sellers was born in Chorley and has lived there most of her life.

She is an ex-President of the Lancashire Caving and Climbing Club, who, for the last forty years, have held an annual walk over the moors that now constitute the West Pennine Moors Recreational Area. Gladys Sellers has been on every one of these walks and it is this knowledge, refined and extended, that forms the basis of this book. She is a retired chemist and has a keen interest in natural history, our environment, and the need to conserve our heritage of moors, pastures and the old farms and villages of the Recreation Area. She is a member of the Lancashire Trust for Nature Conservation.

She has walked, climbed and skied for many years, and amongst the things she has done in the British Isles are: The Pennine Way, The Lakeland 2500 ft tops, The Three Peaks, and the three peaks of the kingdom - Ben Nevis, Scafell Pike and Snowdon - in less than 24 hours. Abroad, she has walked one of the French long distance footpaths through the Maritime Alps, as well as having climbed and skied in France, Switzerland, and Austria. Further afield she has trekked in Kashmir and Nepal.

Since the first edition of this book Gladys Sellers has taken a certificate course on Landscape History at the Extra-Mural Department of the University of Manchester. During this course she made a special study of Anglezarke and White Coppice.

INTRODUCTION

People who live in the immediate vicinity have walked these moors for pleasure for the last 50 years or more, sometimes risking trespass in so doing. Attitudes gradually change, and recently the need for local recreation areas has been accepted. The Water Act of 1973 was an important factor, for it united in a single regional authority the many smaller urban water boards that then existed in the district, and at the same time obliged them to consider possible recreational uses of their land and water. Recognising the importance of Anglezarke, as their chosen area was then called, the Lancashire County Council carried out studies and surveys leading to the publications of a Consultative Report in 1973. After the reorganisation of local government in 1974, the responsibility for developing - or conserving - Anglezarke was divided amongst the two county authorities of Lancashire and Greater Manchester, the borough councils of Blackburn, Chorley, Hyndburn, and Rossendale, and the metropolitan borough councils of Bolton and Bury. They, together with the North West Water Authority, jointly decided to prepare a comprehensive recreational plan. Further surveys and studies were carried out and published, but before preparing a plan of action, they held a number of consultative meetings all around the district to discover what local people thought of their ideas. These meetings were extremely well attended, and some of the ideas the experts put forward were not too well received. People were concerned that their locality should be conserved rather than developed. In particular, the County's original name for the area, Anglezarke, was widely objected to, and the present rather cumbersome title of West Pennine Moors Recreation Area was adopted. In this book it will be abbreviated to Area, and whenever the word is used with a capital A, that is its meaning.

Early in 1978 the Lancashire County Council, on behalf of all the bodies named above, produced its report, 'Approach to a Plan'. This report puts forward the view that in this day and age of the motor car and leisure, the Area will suffer more from the problems of an influx of visitors without a plan than with one. Its Plan aims to give effective management of recreational activities and the traffic they generate, and to conserve and enhance the Area. Any measures introduced to further these aims will be designed so as not to interfere with the farming, forestry, and water catchment, and living conditions in the Area. A difficult requirement indeed! After due regard for the outcome of the public participation meetings the County produced its Draft Plan. There is the possibility of a Public Enquiry, and then the Final Structure Plan can be approved.

The Area covers 90 square miles and its boundaries are roughly as follows: Starting arbitrarily at Horwich, the boundary follows the M61 from a point about 1 mile west of that town to Chorley, where it follows the A674 to Feniscowles. There it turns east along a minor road to Darwen, omits the Darwen urban area, skirts the south of Accrington, and then turns south-east to follow the line of the old railway through Haslingden almost to Ramsbottom, where it turns west a little and follows the B6214 down through Tottington to the B6196 at Ainsworth. From here it takes a devious course round the northern urban fringe of Bolton, excludes Horwich, and finally turns sharply south-west down the B5238 to the M61.

The ground enclosed by the boundaries is predominantly high moorland divided by broad valleys and steep-sided wooded cloughs, many of which contain the reservoirs of the North West Water Authority. This combination of lake, wood, and moor produces scenery that is particularly fine in the western part, and gives some of the best walks, not only in terms of scenery, but of the interesting things to be seen. The widely differing habitats provided by moorlands, streams, and reservoirs means that the Area supports a surprisingly wide range of plants and birds, and the Nature Conservancy Council has designated the Area as a 'Conservation Zone' of country-wide importance.

There is a long history of man's settlement in the Area, not only in the valleys but on the moors themselves. There are a number of interesting remains, ranging from pre-historic monuments to early industrial settlements. On the debit side of man's usage is the large number of mineral workings scattered throughout the Area. Their decline has resulted in some useful terrain for recreation - for example, rock climbing in many of the quarries - but there is much derelict and unsightly ground.

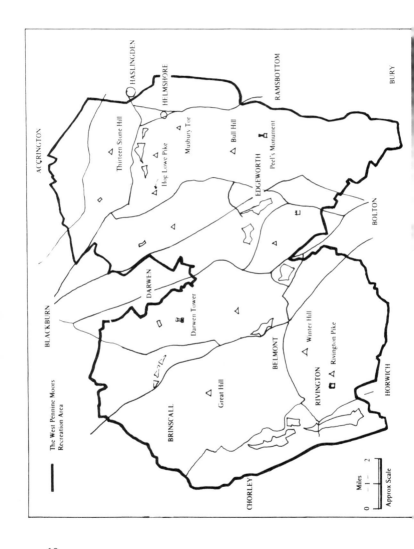

Higher Hill Museum

Part One

THE WEST PENNINE MOORS RECREATION AREA

Introduction

The Implementation of the Draft Plan

The approval of the 'West Pennine Moors Recreation and Conservation Local Plan' by the Secretary of State for the Environment is still awaited because it is a part of the incomplete Structure Plan for the North West. Nevertheless a considerable number of its proposals have now been implemented.

Public consultation had made it abundantly clear that any provision of facilities within the area had to be done with restraint and what might be called 'a minimum package' was prepared. A fundamental need was to resolve the conflicting uses of land for recreation, water catchment, farming, forestry, natural and historic conservation. Four main areas were identified in the early studies as the most frequently visited ones and the provision of facilities for recreation was limited to these four areas. Other types of land use in the rest of the area were given a measure of protection by managing public access, limiting it to existing rights of way. The four areas concerned were dubbed Recreational Management Zones, (RMZ) and they were identified as:

> Rivington
> Jumbles-Wayoh-Entwistle Reservoirs
> Haslingden Grane-Pickup Bank
> Darwen Tower-Roddlesworth

In addition a further nine sites subject to visitor pressure were identified and provision made for them.

Because of differing local opportunities and needs each Zone had its own detailed management plan which includes traffic management. The basic urgent requirement for all Zones, however, was the provision of many more parking areas, some with toilets and picnic places, because studies showed that some 90% of visitors arrived by car. Priorities were established and a good deal of this work has been done. A number of environmental trails have been established and on well-used walking routes stile, footbridge and footpath maintenance work has been done. Much of this work is on land owned by the NWWA and a very large proportion of it has been carried out by Conservation Volunteers based at Tan Pits Farm, Anderton. A start has been made in signposting and waymarking all rights of way and a ranger service has been provided. When the full complement of parking areas has been provided roadside parking will not be permitted and on some roads traffic management schemes will be introduced at busy times.

Within the first three of these areas a great many of the plan's proposals have already been carried out.

Rivington

At Rivington, Great House barn has been converted into a Visitor Information Centre with short stay car park. Here the visitor will find displays about themes such as the building of the reservoirs, a collection of pamphlets about the area, explanations of current work within the Rivington RMZ, a list of birds currently to be seen in the locality. Refreshments are available.

The car park at the Hall Barn has been enlarged and for many walks this is the preferred starting point. Another car park with picnic place and toilets has been made at Middle Derbyshires and others are planned within the Rivington RMZ. Above the Anglezarke Reservoir an area of waste ground has been converted into a car park as has the viewpoint close to Jepson's Farm. The improvement of access and car parking at White Coppice is still awaited. Some improvements of access and car parking at Ward's Reservoir (the Blue Lagoon) at Belmont have been made but there are still more to come. Two environmental trails have been provided but of particular value to the walker has been the replacement of decrepit stiles and bridges and footpath maintenance in popular places.

The Rivington RMZ has had priority in the provision of facilities and most of the changes that have taken place there are within the boundary of Lever Park. In due course this will be extended to include the Pike and Rivington Moor and will be designated a Country Park. In a Country Park recreation is the prime use of the land. When this has been done a new set of right-of-way paths covering many of the existing ones on Anglezarke Moor will be created and the present freedom to wander there will be withdrawn as Anglezarke Moor is not in the RMZ. At present the NWWA is improving some neglected woodland in front of Rivington Hall and restoring the view of the front of the Hall to what it was at the turn of the century.

Jumbles-Wayoh-Entwistle RMZ

The car parking area has been improved and enlarged, toilets provided and refreshments are available at weekends and Wednesday afternoons. There is a small information centre housed in a caravan at present. Some footpath and stile improvement work has been carried out, making possible walks that formerly were not. Noteworthy is the creation of a permissive path of great beauty linking a new car park at Entwistle Reservoir with Wayoh Reservoir. It makes possible a greater choice of walks around the reservoirs. Many of these are not on right-of-way paths but the public is at liberty to use them. An environmental trail has been developed and is fully described in a leaflet avail-

13

able at the Information Office and at Rivington Visitor Centre.

Jumbles is the only Country Park at present within the area and is only a little bigger than the immediate surroundings of Jumbles Reservoir. It was designated a Country Park in 1980.

Haslingden Grane - Pickup Bank

In this RMZ only a small portion around the Grane and Calf Hey Reservoirs has been developed in any way to provide recreational facilities and present intention is to give priority to other land usage in the greater part of the zone. Haslingden Grane is a most unusual area and a trail has been created around the Calf Hey Reservoir which is described in a leaflet giving a great deal of background information about this area. A feature of the trail is the conservation of a few of the ruined houses that abound in this area. Whilst car parking is limited at the start of the trail another much larger car park has been made at Clough Head Quarry and is linked to Calf Hey with new footpaths. An information centre is planned but not as yet provided.

The Rossendale Way goes through the RMZ and the improvement to stiles carried out by Rossendale Groundwork Trust has made practicable a number of walks that formerly were hardly possible and these are included in this volume. As yet nothing has been done at Pickup Bank but it is intended to improve the parking facilities.

Darwen and Roddlesworth

Up to the present little has been achieved within the Darwen -Roddlesworth RMZ except the entension of the small car park at Ryal Fold, Tockholes, and the recent opening up of the paths around the Roddlesworth Reservoirs by the NWWA. A car park is in process of making at Slipper Lowe on the Tockholes road and hopefully will be in use by the summer of 1987. It will give easy access to Darwen Moor and the Wishing Well of Hollinshead Hall, where the ruins are being excavated and treated like those of the Calf Hey Trail. In due course a trail will be made to them from the Slipper Low car park. Darwen Moor is an urban common and there is free access by the public to all of it. Ultimately it is planned to designate Darwen Moor as a Country Park.

1. ROCKS, MINERALS AND MINING

A large number of the rocks of Northern England were formed by material deposited by the Great Upper Carboniferous Delta. This was part of the geological drainage system that operated in the Northern

Hemisphere - for England did not yet exist - some 300 million years ago. It follows that the rocks were all laid down by waterborne particles, that is to say, sand and silt, and have been solidified into rock in the aeons of time that have passed since then. These rocks are broadly classified into Millstone grit, Lower, Upper and Middle Coal Measures. The Coal Measures themselves are a complex sequence of related strata which are repeated several times. These have been classified as fossiliferous shale, barren shale, and mudstone, sandy shale, sandstone, and coal.

Today, after faulting and tilting brought about by earth movements, these rocks are no longer as they were laid down. By means of the fossils present, it has been shown that the rocks of Lester Mill Quarry, Anglezarke, for example, belong to the same strata as some of those that can be seen by the River Roddlesworth at Tockholes, and that they are not the same as those in Healey Nab Quarry, which is very much nearer. The strata have mostly been classified, identified, and named, so that we can refer to the Fletcher Bank grit of Lester Mill Quarry, the Rough Rock of Healey Nab, or the Holcombe Brook coal seam at Rivington. Technically speaking, most of the rock referred to in common speech as 'gritstone' is a modified sandstone.

The melt water streams of the last glacial epoch some 8-9 thousand years ago produced the valley in which the Anglezarke and Rivington Reservoirs were built and the other broad valleys that separate the high moorland blocks of the Area. These valleys have since been modified by the action of the rivers themselves. As the glaciers retreated they left a thick layer of boulder clay on the lower ground, whilst the higher ground, standing above the level of the ice, did not collect this layer.

Having established the geological groundwork, let us consider a little of the detail seen as you walk in the Area. Much of the quarrying and mining that went on, say, a century ago, has ceased. Some deposits such as the coal have been worked out, others have become uneconomic to work, and the Area has a vast legacy of unsightly remains. They do, however, lay bare the bones of the earth to the enquiring mind.

The useful properties of the various layers of sandstone vary considerably. Some contain more coarse particles and are harder than those that contain more of the fine mud and silt particles. These split easily and in times past have been used for paving stones. Quarries tended to work a stone for a particular purpose: at Lester Mill Quarry the stone was mainly for road sets and kerbstones, whilst in the Rossendale valley the Haslingden Flags were used for pavements and roofing stone

One especially pure white gritstone called ganister has been used to line blast furnaces, and fragments can be found in many places round Anglezarke.

Lead and barytes are two other minerals that occur in the Area. Lead was worked in earlier times in three places on Anglezarke moor where there has been faulting and fracturing in the Fletcher Bank Grits. The most important place is in Limestone Clough, locally called Lead Mine Valley, where lead occurs as galena and is accompanied by barytes, witherite, iron pyrites, and some calcite. The vein was at a depth of about 43 yards and was 6-36 inches wide. Mining was carried on here as early as the 17th century and continued until the vein was exhausted. Another vein that was worked is just below Drinkwater Farm on Gt. Hill. At neither place can fragments of galena often be found today - they've all been picked up, but the heavy white barytes (barium sulphate) is still quite plentiful, and in places, so too is witherite (barium carbonate): a relatively rare mineral. Witherite is also very heavy, but is translucent and rather fibrous in appearance.

No less important than the quarrying of stone has been coal mining, now no longer carried out. A small privately owned colliery at Montcliffe, Horwich, was worked up to 1968 though mainly for fireclay. All workable seams are now exhausted. The most important seams are known as the Upper and Lower Mountain seams - indicative of where they were first mined - which was on Darwen and Winter Hills, although the seams cover a much more extensive area. These seams vary in thickness from 2-4ft., and may be found at no great depth, particularly the Upper Mountain Seam. The Lower Mountain Seam outcrops in Stepback Brook, Tockholes, and near the top of the adjacent Cartridge Hill, and was mined there in the middle of the 19th century. Another seam known as the Holcombe Brook Seam outcrops near the Belmont-Rivington road, and at one time was mined to supply Rivington Hall with coal. Today nothing can be seen of these workings, indeed, it is hard to find even fragments of coal, though sizeable pieces can be found around some of the old shafts on Darwen Hill and Moor.

In many places the coal is underlaid by fireclay and this was worked on Smithills and Wilders Moor to make stoneware, and again near Hoddlesden for making glazed bricks. Today the mudstone deposits near Withnell are used for making an engineering brick, and clay at Horwich is used for tile making. Sand deposited by the retreating glaciers' melt water is worked on the fringe of the Area near Chorley. The most recent deposit of all, peat, has been worked near Whittlestone Head, Darwen, for horticultural purposes.

2. MOORLAND PLANTS

Most people think that only grass and heather grow on the moors, or, if they think a bit longer, will add rushes and bilberries to the list. In fact, there's a lot more than that, and it is useful to know a little about them when you are out walking. There's no need to bother with Latin names or anything like that!

If you've done a few of these walks you will probably have noticed that you don't usually get your feet wet when you're going through heather. Everybody knows what heather is like, especially when it's in flower in August, but there is a similar plant called crowberry. This grows in the same sort of dry places as the heather and looks rather like it except that it has much longer spiky leaves and it has little black berries in late summer. They are not poisonous, but it's no pleasure to eat them. Now crowberry, which you can recognise by its bright green mat at all times of the year gives delightful springy walking, quite different from heather, which is often hard work. Bilberry is another plant that likes the same sort of drier place. Bracken likes it drier still. You'll never get your feet wet in a bracken patch!

Having spoken of the plants of the drier places, let us consider those of the wet ones. The really wet ones grow cotton grass, easily recognised by its tuft of 'cotton' just after it has flowered in June. Anywhere you see thick with cotton grass is best avoided unless you're wearing wellies. Another plant of the wet places is purple moor grass: that tall grass that grows into big tussocks. It gives truly abominable walking especially in July and August when its long flower stalks - grasses have flowers, ask any hay fever sufferer - hide the tussocks. There's just one other sort of grass that you might mistake for purple moor grass. It makes smaller tussocks and its leaves are wiry, not flat, and it still likes the wet places. It's called wavy hair grass, and it's probably the commonest grass on the moors. There's another tuft forming plant called mat grass after the mat of decaying yellow leaves that form at its base. It prefers the drier pastures, poor ones at that, and doesn't offer much nourishment for sheep. Otherwise most of the grass isn't grass at all, but sedges and rushes.

Sedges don't only grow round the edges of ponds and lakes: quite a lot of the plants of the wet places in the moors are also sedges. If they're in flower, it is easy to distinguish a sedge from a grass but if not you need to look carefully. The sedges have two quite distinct types of flower on the same stalk, one above the other, and these stalks have a triangular cross-section and they're solid, whereas the flower stalks on grasses are round and hollow. If they're not in flower, look at the leaves. Sedge leaves have a very prominent mid rib giving them a

17

cross-section like a flattened triangle, and a lot of them spread their leaves from a central point in a triangular shape. The difficulties only start if you want to put a name to any particular sedge - the sedges named in this book are probably right, but it's possible they are not!

This may prompt you to wonder what is the difference between a rush and a sedge. Rushes all have round solid stems, and as grasses are round and hollow and sedges triangular and solid there's no real problem. There's more than one sort of rush, though, but the common one all over the moors is the heath rush. It grows spread about like grass, 6-8 inches (15-20cms) high, it has stiff wiry leaves and the 'flower' is a couple of knobbly brown things that last on the plant all winter.

I fear you may be more interested in hearing about pretty and exciting flowers, and want to know why we do not have any on the moors. It's largely because of the nature of the underlying rocks. All wild plants derive their nourishment from the weathering of the rocks which produce the soil and minerals to feed them. The gritstones and shales of our moorland do not produce much mineral matter. In addition the high rainfall 50-60 inches (125-150cms), per annum washes away that which is available almost as it is made. These two factors combine to encourage the production of peat which in turn produces land too acidic to allow the growth of a wide range of plants. a few plants like rhododendron and heather thrive on an acid soil, most others prefer a neutral or limey soil. It so happens that most of our lovely wild flowers like a limey soil, and we haven't got one in this area. That's why there's so few harebells in our hedgerows and why we have the white bedstraw instead of the yellow bedstraw that grows around Malham. There are just a few places in the Area where some lovely wildflowers can be found, but until the general public are happy to see these flowers where they grow and not to pick them by the wilting handful, then these places must remain known only to the naturalists.

3. PRE-HISTORY OF THE MOORS

The archaeological remains in the Area are probably more numerous than one would think: at the same time they are probably smaller and less interesting than one would have hoped. This part of England never had the wealth of archaeological remains that exist in the south of England, and of those there are, many have been damaged or even destroyed. Our small remains are best appreciated with some knowledge of the general pattern of pre-history, defined as anything that happened before writing was in use. In Great Britain this art was brought over by the Romans, so pre-history starts with the very earliest man, possibly 500,000 B.C., and ends at about 50 A.D.

It must be made clear at the beginning that dates used in pre-history are necessarily very vague. Not only is there the difficulty in putting a date to any place or object (and the older the greater the problem) but in addition, when talking about the end of the New Stone Age and the start of the Bronze Age, for example, this does not mean that it was clean cut and sharp. It simply means that fewer stone axes and scrapers were used as they were gradually replaced by bronze ones. Furthermore, ideas travelled very slowly and as new cultures generally came from the continent to the south of England, changes are likely to have taken place there possibly centuries before the same changes took place in the north of England.

The very earliest men, the Old Stone Age men, were hunters and collectors of berries and herbs. They lived in caves and used massive stone hand axes, that is to say, a shaped and sharpened stone held in the hand. None of their remains have been found in the Area. The oldest remains in the Area are the microliths made by Mesolithic Man or Middle Stone Age Man, dated variously 8000-12,000 B.C. These microliths have been found on **Bull Hill** and other places, though on Bull Hill there have been so many that a chipping floor or workshop is thought to have been sited there. Though very small, roughly the size of a finger nail, technically they are a great advance on the hand axe as they were made to set in a bone or wooden handle which has long since disappeared. These people were hunters and food collectors like their ancestors.

By about 3500 B.C. agriculture, discovered in the Middle East as early as 10,000 B.C. had arrived in southern Britain, and the farmers of the New Stone Age, Neolithic Man became established. Neolithic Man buried his dead in long barrows. Where these survive intact, as they do in some parts of the country, they are mounds of earth some 150ft. long and 60ft. wide, but if the earth covering has been removed or weathered away, then the inner stone burial chamber is exposed. Pike Stones is thought to be one of these and to have been built between 3000 and 2000 B.C. It is the oldest man-made object of any size in the area. It is the remains of a five slab burial chamber and stands on a low egg shaped mound of packed stones 160ft. long and 60ft. wide. Originally the chambered tomb would have been earth covered. The outline can be quite easily seen except in summer when the long grass veils it. At the wider end this ring of packed stones curves round like a pair of horns to make a forecourt where ritual

Pike Stones

could have been carried out in front of the entrance. Many of the dolmens or cromlechs found in South Wales and South West England are similar structures.

The New Stone Age very gradually merged into the Early Bronze Age for which a nominal date of 1600 B.C. has been given. The Early, Middle and Late Bronze Ages lasted 1,000 years and were ultimately replaced by the Iron Age in around 500 B.C. This period of 1,000 years has left quite a number of characteristic tumuli or round barrows in the Area. Around 1500 B.C. there was a marked improvement in climate. It became drier and warmer. Evidence for this has been obtained from examination of pollen obtained from the deep layers of peat. Every sort of pollen grain is quite characteristic of the plant that produces it, and it can be recognised under the microscope. Very fortunately the outer skin of pollen grains is an exceedingly tough and durable materials and pre-historic pollen grains have survived in the peat on the moor. These grains belong to birches, alders, and oaks which won't grow on the moors in today's climate. It is quite clear that the better climate enabled the Bronze Age men to live, die and be buried on the moors, for practically the only remains of them is their burial mounds, a number of which were to be found on the moors. Excavation by both Victorian treasure hunters and later archaeologists has resulted in little more than their sites being visible today. Originally they were round mounds some 50ft. in diameter and the earth was retained by a circle of large stones. In the middle was a stone chamber or cist where burial urns holding cremated remains were placed. When Noon Hill was excavated in the 1950's there was evidence of four burials. Scrapers, arrow heads and an urn were found. These are now housed in Bolton Municipal Museum. Pottery in particular enables dates to be assigned rather more accurately and 2000-1400 B.C. has been suggested for this tumulus, and the one on **Winter Hill** is of a similar date. Very little can be seen today of either of these mounds. Excavation is a destructive process. A mound in the grounds of **White Hall,** Over Darwen, was excavated late last century, and evidence of ten Bronze Age burials was found. Three pottery urns have been restored and are displayed in the Reference Library at Darwen.

The Twa Lads on the moor of that name were a pair of these Bronze Age burial mounds. Standing Stones on Anglezarke Moor were the remains of another cairn. The remains of the circle of stones on Chetham Close is thought to be the outer ring of a Bronze Age cairn.

One way of dating a find of any sort is to compare it and the place where it was found with other finds and sites about which more is known. Pottery is very useful because it is reasonably durable even though early pieces were not so well fired as present day pottery. Its shape and above all its decoration help to date it. There were fashions even then. Radio carbon dating is of limited value in dating these early finds. A substantial amount of carbonaceous material is needed for the test, and so often there isn't enough, or any at all.

Very few Bronze Age tools have been found compared with the number of flint tools. The latter became blunt very rapidly and were no doubt then discarded. Bronze was a valuable substance that could be re-melted, and though bronze tools may have been lost, it is unlikely that they were ever thrown away.

Around 500 B.C. settlers from Europe using superior iron tools and

Round Loaf, with Great Hill behind 21

weapons invaded this country. They speedily overran the existing population and thus the Celtic Iron Age was established. At the same time the climate changed and became colder and wetter, and the Iron Age men were the first to wear trousers. Villages and field patterns developed as agriculture became established as the way of life rather than hunting - not that they were peaceable people, far from it, for their chief remain is the hill fort. Again this was most highly developed in the south of England, and Maiden Castle is the best example. The Druidic culture dates from this period. Little is known of the religion of these people who were driven westwards into Wales by the Romans, and today's Druidic rites are largely the invention of the romantic minds of the mid 18th century. What little evidence there is suggests that the Druids formed a body of essential knowledge such as the working of the calendar, medicine, religious practices and poetry.

As the Romans gradually subdued the country after their successful invasion, they brought with them the new skill of writing. Pre-history in England was coming to an end. The Romans built a network of roads to connect the forts they built to subdue the country. In Lancashire the best known fort was at Ribchester and it was connected to the one at Manchester by Watling Street, which runs through the Area from Starling near Bury through Affetside, Edgworth, and Grimehills to the outskirts of Blackburn. Today there is nothing to be seen of the road above ground. Excavations in the 1950's near **Bottom o' Knotts Brow,** Turton, revealed a portion of road. More recent excavations near **Pallet Farm,** Edgworth, laid bare another portion. Both these excavations were filled in again. The bridge across the stream below the **Crown and Thistle Inn,** Grimehills, is reputedly of Roman origin. There have been finds of coins in various places, but regretfully, there is virtually nothing else left.

4. THE HISTORY OF THE ANGLEZARKE
MOORLAND FARMS

In common with most of the moorland fringes of Lancashire quite a number of ruined farmhouses are to be found on the moors of Anglezarke. In most of these areas the land was settled - farmhouses built and the fields enclosed from the surrounding waste land - during the first part of the eighteenth century, but in Anglezarke that process was started many centuries earlier. The first settlers here were the Irish -Norse in the ninth or tenth century, for the name Anglezarke is derived from a Norse personal name, Anlaf, and the word ending --argh, which means a summer shielding or saeter. In old documents the name Anglezarke is written as Andlesargh or Anlesargh, even as late as the nineteenth century. Norse derived place names are common along the Lancashire coast - Kirkby, Crosby, Birkdale to name but a few, and all of them, like Anglezarke, were first settled by Norsemen from either Ireland or the Isle of Man.

Little is known of Anglezarke until the start of the 17th century when a document in the Lancashire Record Office dated 1623 states that the Manor of Anglezarke had, amongst other things, 12 houses with gardens. Clearly a great deal of settling of the land had already taken place and there is reason to believe that settlement had already been going on slowly for around 400 years. The Manor of Anglezarke belonged to the Standish family from 1623-1897 but it did not comprise the whole of the township*, even though it extended to Deane Brook at White Coppice and included two farms there. A considerable portion of land belonged to the Shaws of Hall o'th' Hill who owned four more farms in Anglezarke including Manor House. The name Manor House is a Victorian affectation. The house's true name is High Bullough, for Bullough is an ancient family name in Anglezarke. In the eighteenth century there were three other farms with the family name Bullough - Wilkinson Bullough, Gernest Bullough and Parson's Bullough. All of them are shown on the 6″ to the mile O.S. map of 1847 and some are on the current 1:25,000 map. All these farms were located on the lower land around the Anglezarke Reservoir, then a marshy valley, and in the lower part of the valley of the River Yarrow. The three farms at the head of the Yarrow were built much later, in the first quarter of the eighteenth century. Of these 19 farms only five including the two at White Coppice are now occupied and not necessarily by a farming family. The rest are ruins, some just a few stones barely visible in long grass.

Thanks to the practice of listing a man's possessions at his death up to about 1730, a fair amount is known about the people of Anglezarke and how they made a living in the 17th century. All of them grew oats which were ground into meal at the Manor Corn Mill and used for making clap bread, (a thin wafer-like oat cake) or porridge. The ploughing was done by teams of oxen. Most men owned 2 or 4 oxen and everybody owned a number of cattle, usually between 4 and 12, mostly milkers, and butter and cheese were made. Many of them kept between 40 and 100 sheep, and most people owned a horse or two, farm implements, carts and pack saddles but only one hackney saddle is recorded in the whole 140 year period covered by these inventories. Men walked about their business. A few geese are recorded - geese are grass eaters, but no other poultry and no pigs. Livestock was grazed

*A township is a part of a parish   23

Old Rachel's, a derelict farm on the moor

on the open ground above the fields and there was insufficient good land to grow enough hay to keep more than a nucleus of animals through the winter. Most would be killed off in the late autumn and salted. A vat for this purpose is recorded in one inventory, as these lists of property were called. Another house had a vat for brewing beer -there was no tea in those days. All the houses had chairs and stools, but strangely, no tables. It was common practice to place a few boards on a pair of trestles. Most of them had settles, some with cushions. All of them had beds, a few with linen sheets and feather pillows. People no longer slept in a heap on the floor. In the kitchens there were fire irons, frying pans, pewter and brass pots, and presumably many lesser items not recorded. A few households scattered through the years had spinning wheels, even fewer had hand looms. Only one man in the inventories could be described as a handloom weaver. He was a John Shaw who lived at Stones House and died in 1686. All in all the people of Anglezarke were quite comfortably off. There was plenty of borrowing and lending, and there must have been a fair amount of bartering, for this was before the days of banking and a cash economy.

By the end of the first quarter of the eighteenth century the winds of change were blowing: the years of self sufficiency were ending.

Ploughing diminished and more livestock was kept, particularly sheep. People were moving in to the towns to seek a better living there as corn growing is a labour intensive process compared with sheep rearing. By this time the three farms at the head of the Yarrow valley, Simms, Higher and Lower Hempshaws were established. At this time this lower part of the moor was not moorland but rough grass and heather. Its deterioration to cotton grass and purple moor grass - both having a very low nutritional value for animals - has taken place in the last 100 years or so. The great field between Simms and Lower Hempshaws, scarcely recognisable as a field today, was a hay meadow at the turn of this century.

Farming continued to follow this general pattern, supplemented by a certain amount of handloom weaving, until the 1880's. The building of the reservoirs in 1855 had undoubtedly caused problems to the farming community. Some of them lost land and Lester Mill, the Manor Corn Mill, by then a farm and no longer a corn mill, had disappeared under the waters of the Anglezarke Reservoir. However, all of them continued to farm. By 1880 British farming was in the throes of a depression due to cheap imports of corn. Some of the smaller farms were amalgamated, for they had usually no more than 30 acres and in some cases as few as 8, and rents were reduced. Men obtained jobs in the quarries and mills of Adlington, and many became part-time farmers.

Liverpool Corporation, who had followed a policy of buying up land whenever it came onto the market in order to carry out their mandate to provide a pure water supply, bought the remaining land from its current owner, a Mr. Mayhew, in 1904. There is no evidence that they evicted the remaining tenants of Anglezarke but as leases were on an annual basis it was easy to bring pressure to bear upon the tenants to move out of farming. By degrees everybody sold up and the whole of Anglezarke was vacated by 1907. It stayed vacant until 1911 when all the land was amalgamated in the one holding of Manor House, where the present tenant, Mr. Drinkall has followed his father. He now farms some 3,000 acres and keeps 200 head of beef cattle and about 2,000 sheep. Modern farming methods enable him to grow sufficient hay to keep the cattle throughout the winter.

In the last five years or so a number of shelter belts of trees have been planted, notably close to Pikestones and on the moor above Simms. At present these are a mixture of conifers and our native hardwoods, mainly alder, rowan, birch and oak. When the slow growing hardwoods have become well established, the conifers, having done their job to provide shelter for the young hardwood trees, will be felled. There will then be plantations of our native British trees such as have not been seen on these moors since late Bronze Age times. It is expected that their falling leaves will slowly build up the fertility of the ground and by providing shelter for livestock there will be further slow gains in fertility.

5. ANCIENT MONUMENTS AND MUSEUMS

There are eleven scheduled Ancient Monuments including three museums that are protected by the 1913-1953 Acts. These Ancient Monuments comprise the three museums, five pre-historic burial mounds, two headless crosses and a portion of Roman road. Except the museums, which are very fine buildings indeed, none of the Ancient Monuments are very impressive and not all are worth a special visit. The policy of the Department of the Environment is to schedule a site even if it has been excavated and covered in again. This goes some way to ensure that it is protected against destruction or damage, and this is the case as far as the Roman road at the Bottom o' Knotts Brow, Turton is concerned. It was excavated in the 1950's, established as genuine, and filled in again. Similarly, at the tumulus on Winter Hill, little can be seen today.

The burial mounds are all remote from any road and are visited on the following walks:

Round Loaf, Anglezark   Walk No.1.10, Section 1
Pike Stones, Anglezarke   Walk No.1.10, Section 1
Noon Hill Ring Cairn, Winter Hill   Walk No.1.1 No. 4 to 1.5,
                                                        Section 1

Round Barrow on Winter Hill   Walk No.1.5, Section 1
Stone Circles on Chetham Close   Walk No.2.5, Section 2

Some notes about them are at the end of the relevant walk. In addition there is more information about them in the previous chapter on the pre-history of the moors.

The **Headless Cross** at Anderton is by the roadside at a crossroads on a minor road behind the Millstone Hotel, Horwich, which is at the northern end of the reservoir embankment on the A673. Tradition says that the figure on it is St. Anthony. When so many crosses lost their heads during the reign of Henry VIII and Edward VI the pillars were sometimes put to other uses. In due time this one became a signpost pointing the way to Blegburn, (note the spelling), Bolton, Wigan, and Preston. Fairly obviously the lettering is not nearly as old as the rest of the cross. During the building of the Anglezarke and

Affetside - Headless Cross

Rivington reservoirs, the cross was removed from its traditional place and eventually found its way to Viscount Leverhulme's Bungalow Gardens. The Lancashire County Council restored it to its present position in 1945. The two-position stocks were there at that time.

The **Headless Cross** at Affetside stands by the road in the village, the approximate site of the Roman road, Watling Street. It is, at the moment, the only one of these Ancient Monuments bearing the plate of H.M. Office of Works indicating that it is an Ancient Monument. The Lancashire and Cheshire Antiquarian Society investigated it in the early years of this century. They considered it to be the remains of a Market Cross, possibly from Jacobean times, indicating a nearby field where a market was held.

The three museums, Smithills Hall, Turton Tower, and Higher Mill are all quite different from each other both as far as the buildings themselves are concerned and their dispays. Higher Mill is unique, being devoted to early cotton manufacturing processes. Hall i' th' Wood is another museum only just outside the Area, and having strong associations with the Industrial Revolution, is worth a visit before visiting Higher Mill Museum.

27

Smithills Hall

Smithills Hall, Bolton

Lies just off the B6207 where that road crosses the Moss Bank Way ring road, the A58. It is well signposted. A bus runs direct to the Hall from Bolton town centre. The hall is a large complex structure of various periods, much of it in black and white work, but only a relatively small part, the oldest, is open to the public. The oldest of all, the Great Hall, is all that remains of a manor house thought to be older than 1350, and one of the oldest in Lancashire. It has been carefully restored and sparsely furnished in the style of the times. Much more ornate, and in great contrast to the austerity of the Great Hall, is the East Wing, added in Henry VIII's reign. This is a truly beautiful room, whose walls are lined with fine linen-fold panelling. It is appropriately furnished and gives a picture of gracious living. Of considerable local interest are the pictures of old Bolton lining the main corridors.

A little distance away is the old coach house and stables, now used as a restaurant. They are Grade 2 listed buildings. The whole of the buildings are surrounded by fine lawns and gardens backed by woodland, where there is a nature trail. Even better in wet weather is a nature trail cabin, where a series of photographs, diagrams, pressed leaves and grasses, mounted birds, insects and mammals show all the things that might be seen on the trail, together with a geologically based explanation. The whole is extremely well done, and a whole afternoon can be spent there.

Turton Tower

Turton Tower, Bolton

Turton Tower is of a rather different character from Smithills and is a Grade 1 listed building. It lies just off the B6391 a few hundred yards south of Chapeltown, is signposted and there is a bus stop at the door. Parking is within the grounds of the Tower itself. You usually drive right up to the Tower, feeling very grand, before turning right into the car park.

The Tower is quite an impressive structure dating from 1400 A.D. It is built around an ancient 'pele tower', a type of fortified house fairly common in the North of England and usually built as a means of defence against the raiding Scots in the time of Robert the Bruce. Later on the fine looking black and white farmhouse was added by the Orrell family, and in 1596 a William Orrell raised the height of the tower in order to increase the height of the rooms in it. This can be seen quite clearly. Humphrey Chetham, of Chetham's Hospital fame, is the Tower's most famous owner. It changed hands a number of times after his ownership and was finally given to the Turton U.D.C. by the widow of Sir Lees Knowles in 1930. Today it is cared for by the Lancashire County Council. At present the building is open Saturday to Wednesday 12-5.00p.m. Entry costs seventy pence. Inside there are some fine pieces of carved oak furniture, some of them from Bradshaw Hall, now demolished. The conference room is pleasant, but somehow too modern to be in-keeping with a pele tower. Only this room and the

29

dining room seem to be as they were, rooms for living in, as opposed to rooms for displaying collections of furniture or other articles. The top room of the tower is in this latter category although it really looks the part of a fortified house. It has bare stone walls, a collection of swords and suits of armour on the walls, stags heads and hunting horns. This first impression of character is unfortunately spoiled by the ceiling, obviously modern and quite out of keeping with the rest of the room. The Tower was re-roofed about twenty years ago and no heed seems to have been paid to doing the job in harmony with the rest of the building.

If you wander along the little footpath in front of the Tower, you will come to a stone barn by the side of which is the restored water-wheel from Black Rock Mill. This was a cotton spinning mill, print and bleach works that stood on Bradshaw Brook just above the bridge at Turton Bottoms. The wheel supplied the power from roughly 1850-1900. Turton Local History Society did the restoration work.

Museum of the Lancashire Textile Industry and Higher Mill Museum

The Higher Mill Museum site has now been augmented by the acquisition of the adjacent three storey stone built spinning mill. This building now houses a major display showing the development of the textile industry in Lancashire, and gives demonstrations of the spinning mules as used 100 years ago. Higher Mill Museum, a museum with a difference, continues substantially as before. There's none other even remotely like it in the Area, nor even in the whole of Lancashire. It is a late eighteenth century fulling mill in working order - incredible! (Fulling is the final processing given to woollen cloth such as is used for blankets.) The mill lies on the B6235 road which links the B6232 and the B6215 roads on the south-west side of Haslingden. It has a signpost at the entrance and is not hard to find, though its closeness to another old mill is at first puzzling. Just drive in.

The building itself, recently renovated, makes two sides of a court-yard, and dating from 1789, looks very fine indeed. The ground floor is open Monday to Friday, 2.00 p.m. to 5.00 p.m. except in November, December, January and February. It is open at other times in the summer months. Admission costs seventy pence which covers both buildings. This is the original part of the fulling mill and contains fulling machinery made in the early years of the nineteenth century and was worked by a water-wheel right up to 1954. The water-wheel has been restored and the banks of the reservoir strengthened, so the wheel can be worked for visitors. It is not, however, geared up to the machinery as it used to be, and some of that is demonstrated for you by means of an electric motor.

Upstairs there is a collection of cotton spinning machinery, including early examples of Arkwright's water frame and Hargreaves' spinning jenny. These are all in working order and are demonstrated to parties who have booked a tour. Unfortunately the danger from primitive shafts and belts to people are such that this machinery can only be demonstrated to people on a guided tour. This must be pre-booked, and costs at present £1 per person with a minimum of £10. Parties must not exceed 20 people. Ring the Museum Manager (Rossendale 226459) for an appointment.

The potential of this building, not just the museum of exhibits, but as a demonstration of cotton manufacture as it used to be carried out, is extremely high. If you or your family have ever been in the cotton industry, you'll find it particularly fascinating.★

★Remains of the cotton industry abound in the Area (see next chapter). Examples of machinery are displayed at the Textile Machinery Museum, Tonge Moor Library, Tonge Moor Road, Bolton.

Hall i' th' Wood, Bolton

Lies off the A58 ring road between the A575 and the A676. It can just be seen a few hundred yards away on the north side of the ring road

Hall I'th'Wood

and is approached through a housing estate. It is signposted, but not quite so well as Smithills Hall.

Hall i' th' Wood is yet another of Viscount Leverhulme's benefactions. He bought it in 1897 whilst he was still Mr. Lever and gave it to Bolton Corporation together with sufficient money for its restoration, for it was then in bad condition. The Hall's main claim to fame is that it is the place where Samuel Crompton was living when he invented the spinning mule in 1779; one of the most important inventions of the Industrial Revolution. Not that Crompton was one of the aristocracy, far from it. He was just one of a family of weavers who occupied the building with other families and farmers. As is fitting in such a building, much of its furniture is of a homely nature. There is a huge fireplace with an equally huge spit turned by an ingenious arrangement of stone weights, cheese presses, clothes presses, coffee mills turned by hand, goffer irons and all manner of long forgotten domestic items. One room is devoted to Crompton's possessions and things connected with him. There is a spinning-wheel he used as a child, a violin and an organ he made, pictures of his parents, his letters seeking financial backing for his invention, but rather disappointingly, only a small model of the mule itself. As a contrast to the grandeur of nearby Smithills Hall, it's very well worth a visit at the same time.

6. CONSERVATION AREAS

Conservation Areas do much to enhance the character of any particular region. In the years before cheap transport and universally available building materials made architectural styles deadly uniform, local geological structures limited the materials available and climate defined the style. Few houses and factories were built in other than this manner and thus architectural character was established. Every generation decries the efforts of its immediate predecessors as old fashioned and worthless, and so demolition has been the order of the day. However, over the last twenty years public opinion has changed from this view to one that seeks to find and preserve the best examples that are left. Thus has come into being the concepts of the Conservation Area and the listed building. These ideas have been given legal backing by the Country Amenities Act of 1974 which requires local authorities to designate Conservation Areas and to take steps to preserve and enhance their character. A listed building is one of architectural or historic interest, and again is subject to the control of the local authority. These buildings include every type - farms, houses, mills, pubs, churches and monuments, and are graded by their quality. The standards for a Grade 1 building are very high, and there are only four of them within the Area. They are Smithills Hall, Rivington Hall Barn, Great House Barn, and Turton Tower. Grade 2 and 2A buildings are too numerous to list, but some outstanding ones are mentioned in the text of this book. Where many of these listed buildings occur together, that little area has a character all of its own, and it is areas like these that have been designated Conservation Areas. Some of these areas include considerable tracts of countryside such as at Wallsuches. There are no notice boards to indicate the areas, nor any boundary marks. The observer must have a map and an appreciative eye.

Most of the Conservation Areas are either close to starting points of walks or are passed through during the course of a walk. Few are worth a special visit unless you are especially interested in local architecture and conservation. Here are a few notes about them in alphabetical order.

Abbey Village, Chorley, was built around and was totally dependant on a weaving mill, and even as late as December 30th, 1971, the last day the mill ran, there was no other employment in the village. It was built during the hey-day of the Industrial Revolution in 1846, and the original mill cottages that line Bolton Road make a fine avenue. Many are being modernised and the mill has found new uses. The village stands on the Bolton-Preston road, the A675, and can be usefully visited during Walk No.5, Section 4.

Ainsworth, Radcliffe, is a village with a degree of isolation and has retained its identity. The main road used to run in front of the pub, the Duke William. In those days it was an old coaching inn, still with its high doorway that would admit a coach to the rear. Close at hand is the Unitarian Chapel built in 1715 and enlarged and rebuilt through the years, but full of character. Its graveyard has possibly the best collection of old gravestones, many prior to 1800, in the Area. The Parish Church is not especially noteworthy, being largely rebuilt in early Victorian times, but just inside its lichgate is a pair of stumps that were once part of the village stocks. There are several rows of cottages still in good repair that keep the old village character intact. The village stands on the B6196, Bury to Bradshaw road.

Barrow Bridge, Bolton, is the site of one of the early 'model villages' of industrial Lancashire. It was founded in 1846 by Thomas Bazley,

33

and the two spinning mills, long since demolished, employed 800 people. They were housed in the model village of which the curiously named Second, Third, Fourth, and Fifth Streets remain. These lie on Bazley Road up the hill from the bus stop. The school, Mechanics Institute, and a number of other old houses lie on it. Quite a number of these as well as the fine old houses in Barrow Bridge Road are Grade 2 listed buildings. Reverting to a bit more history, the mill changed hands and in 1876 the new owner died. The mills closed and the inhabitants had to seek work elsewhere. In the closing years of this century Barrow Bridge became a deserted village. Now the wheel of fortune has changed. Old mill cottages have become much sought after homes for all sorts of people. Still writing of mills, the prominent chimney at the junction of Moss Lane is listed as a Grade 2 building. One would hardly say that it is beautiful, but there are not many of them left, and chimneys are a very essential part of the Lancashire scene. Barrow Bridge is the starting point for Walk No.8, Section 2, and is best approached from the Moss Bank Way ring road, Bolton, A58, bearing left all the time from Moss Bank Park traffic lights.

Chapeltown, Bolton, is only about ½ mile from Turton Bottoms and Edgworth and they can quite easily be visited together. The whole of the village street is attractive, but the finest part lies at the northern end. The pub, the Chetham Arms, is a Grade 2 listed building as are also a number of houses in the High Street. A little further on is a little garden set aside to house the old market cross and village stocks. It is a pleasant corner with some new garden seats. The village lies on the B6391 which leaves the A660 Bolton-Darwen road at Bromley Cross.

Chatterton and Strongstry, Rossendale. These two places are hardly villages, just rather isolated rows of stone-built weavers cottages on the banks of the River Irwell. At Chatterton the mill remains as well. There is quite a rural atmosphere about the place and they are best visited by a short (30-40 min.) walk from Stubbins. Start at the Railway Hotel, go under the railway bridge, and turn right. Continue along the road leading to Stubbins Vale Mill and follow it until you come to the old railway on your right. Go under the bridge and just ahead on your left is the double row of cottages of Strongstry. Continue along the pleasant riverside path to the first footbridge, cross it and continue along the minor road through the hamlet of Chatterton until you meet the A56. Turn left on it and a few minutes will see you back to your starting point. Stubbins lies on the A676 just north of Ramsbottom.

Edgworth, Bolton. The Conservation Area in this long drawn out village is at the bottom of the hill, near Turton Bottoms, not where the name Edgworth appears on the map. The bulk of the houses are up the hill, and there are a number of very fine old ones, such as those in Isherwood Fold, and Brandwood Fold, built in 1650, but the village atmosphere is diminished by the large housing estate. Lower down along Bolton road are the pub, the Spread Eage, the old Methodist School built in 1828, and a large number of other Grade 2 listed buildings. Though very extended, Edgworth probably has as many fine buildings and interesting 'corners' as anywhere in the Area. It stands on a minor road that runs from the B6391 at Chapeltown to B6232 Blackburn-Haslingden road.

Hoddlesden, Darwen. This hilltop village built around Queens Street and Queens Square owes its present form to the twin Victorian pillars of coal and cotton. Once the centre of a considerable colliery activity, it had a special branch-line built from the Darwen-Bolton railway line to transport its coal. Today just a fragment can be seen at the bottom of the hill. Two of its old mills remain, still in use. The village's principal attraction lies in its compactness and its freedom from modern intrusion. Perhaps the most attractive feature is the pair of symmetrically gabled rows of houses in a late Georgian style bearing words in Latin: *BUILT BY O.HARGREAVE, 1844.* Holker House Farm is worth a short walk to look at. Park by the Congregational Church and turn left before the road climbs steeply up to the village. Turn left at the next T junction, and the house is in sight about 100 yards away. Time: 5-10 minutes. From this point you can see the remains of the railway track that went up to the colliery on Grey Stone Hill. Can be approached along minor roads from either Darwen or Blackburn.

Holcombe, Ramsbottom. The area included here is quite large and extends up to the Monument on the moor. The most picturesque corner lies along the bridleway, lined with elegant old houses, rather than weavers cottages. Further along the bridleway is Hey House and the Aitken Sanatorium, formerly Holcombe Hall. Walk No.3, Section 3, takes you through this area. It lies along the old Haslingden-Bury road, B6214.

Irwell Vale, Rossendale. The Rossendale valley, the once beautiful valley of the River Irwell, ravaged in the early days of the Industrial Revolution, here retains something of its rural charm. Situated at the

Holcombe

end of the road between the R. Irwell and the R. Ogden, there is little room for development and the community of mill workers cotages has stayed intact. It is best approached from Ewood Bridge on the A680 Haslingden-Ramsbottom road.

Riding Gate, Harwood, Bolton. This quaint corner is not named on the map as such, it's really a street name, but it is very close to Side of the Moor which is shown on the map. In an area swamped with new housing estates this road contrives to retain an air of seclusion and contains some fine large houses. The Conservation Area includes a fair amount of the pastures around. It is best reached by taking the Tottington road from the B6196 at Harwood Lee and turning left just past the Methodist Chapel.

Wallsuches, Horwich. The Conservation Area takes it name from the former bleach works, but it is more extensive than one would at first suppose. The former bleach works are now occupied by an engineering firm and have recently been cleaned and painted. Bleach works were once a common and important part of the Lancashire scene, many have fallen into disuse and become completely ruinous. This one, thanks to a new use, has been well cared for. Some of the buildings, in particular the old engine house, are impressively designed and built. A date stone on the mill gives a date of 1858. A right of way footpath runs through the centre of the buildings and they can easily be inspected on a short walk.

Park in the lay-by opposite the Jolly Crofters, which lies on the B6226, the Bolton-Horwich old road. Take the cinder track past a short row of stone cottages. One of them has the date 1803. The track continues through the works, passing what looks like the original manager's or owner's house. It meets another track coming up from Horwich and which leads to a metalled road and some modern houses. Turn right here and follow it past the reservoir banking. Here is a very fine house indeed, Markland House, with a date stone 1773. Turn right on the footpath here and follow it past some small reservoirs to the cinder track that takes you back to your car in a couple of minutes. Time: 30-40 minutes.

7. THE INDUSTRIAL HISTORY OF WHITE COPPICE

Few visitors to White Coppice would ever imagine that 150 years ago this tiny rural hamlet was a busy industrial village having a population of around 180 people. During the first 50 or so years of the Industrial Revolution all machines were water powered and sites at the foot of the moors were in demand. In Lancashire the Industrial Revolution is generally considered to have started between the years 1770 and 1780, following the invention of Hargreaves' spinning jenny in 1764, Arkwright's water frame in 1770 and Crompton's mule in 1779. These machines speeded up the production of yarn for weaving enormously and ended the bottleneck that slowed down the production of cloth. The application of water power to the loom came much later as it is a more complex mechanism. Most early factories were therefore spinning mills but even earlier than the spinning mills were bleach and dye works, for these processes need chemicals and cauldrons of hot water and were ill suited to the domestic hearth. It seems likely therefore, that the first industrial process at White Coppice would be one or the other of these.

Before the Industrial Revolution White Coppice was known as Warth - the modern name only seems to have come into use about 1840. The hamlet lies partly in Heapey and partly in Anglezarke and the stream is the boundary between them. There are two estate maps in the Lancashire Records Office showing the hamlet of Warth in 1774 as having just three houses, (one of them Warth Farm, still to be seen close to the bridge) and two farms, Coppice and Gerrards, on the Anglezarke side of the stream. Northwood and the Shieling are much more recent buildings.

The first indication that there was some sort of industry at White Coppice is found in a lease of Coppice Farm dated 1801. There is a clause to the effect that the occupant 'must not injure the flow of water to the Warth Factory'. Where was the factory and what did it do? We can only guess, for there is not another word until 1810 when another document states that 'The Coppice Bleachers have purchased the lease of the Mill and Mill Croft'. Was this the Warth Factory? The mill referred to was almost certainly the Manor Corn Mill, known to have been in existence as long ago as 1623. The Mill Croft is shown on the estate map and lay roughly behind the cottages facing the cricket field, but the mill is not shown. It is possible that the Coppice Bleachers were indeed the occupants of the Warth factory and needing new premises, had moved to the disused Manor Corn Mill. Equally they may have already been in occupation of the corn mill and were merely consolidating their position. Bleaching and dyeing continued in White Coppice at least until 1835. It is not clear where the factory was except it was on the Anglezarke side of the stream and it may not necessarily have occupied the site of the Manor Corn Mill. Our knowledge of these early years is very fragmented and incomplete.

Another early bleach works close to Warth was known as the Shackerley Factory. There is a reference to it dated 1813. Shackerley is the name of a house, recently restored, that stands above the lowest of the three lodges (Nos.1, 2 and 3) that lie between the scrap steel works at Heapey and White Coppice. (Walk No.1.13 goes past them.) Presumably the factory was close by in the valley bottom as these lodges were not yet built. By 1841 this factory was known as Heapey Bleach Works. By 1851 there was another small bleach works known as Pendlebury's Bleach Works just above it and four small lodges in the valley supplied their water. It is not known when these lodges were enlarged to make the present Nos.1, 2 and 3 lodges, possibly when Heapey Bleach Works was taken over by Dacca Twist in 1880, but it was certainly done by 1893. By this time all the lodges at White Coppice had been built. The first one to be built was the Old Mill Pond, (No.8 lodge) probably in the early years of the nineteenth century. Evidently it was not big enough to supply the growing needs and at some unknown date, certainly before 1841, it was backed up by another that tapped Black Dean Brook. The path to Great Hill passes beneath its embankment and the breach in its wall marks the place where the sluice gates were mounted. They controlled the flow of water to the Old Mill pond below through a wooden flume or launder. When the Goit was built in 1855 it was destroyed.

Sometime between 1835 and 1841 White Coppice Cotton Mill was established by Ephraim Cocker, a Darwen man whose family was connected with India Mill, Darwen. He came to live at Coppice Farm and built Northwood, or Albion Villa as it was then called. His mill wove calico and muslins and in 1851 employed 43 men, 48 women, 11 boys and 15 girls. Its looms were water powered and the water-wheel took water from the lodge (No.4) immediately above it. It was lit by gas which was made on the premises, and later used to raise steam. A separate lodge was made to supply this water, the small one in the field below Northwood, and water was led to the mill by the roadside ditch still visible today. In the 1880's the mill was managed by A.E.Eccles who was a fervent teetotaller and non-smoker and who 'ruled' White Coppice, obliging his work-force to comply with his ideas. When the mill closed in 1914 it had 40 looms, and it was demolished sometime in the 1920's. Today only traces of the buildings remain, lost in nettles and sapling trees.

Obviously a work-force of the size employed in 1851 would require many more houses than the few shown on the estate maps of 1774. The Row and the cottages by the cricket field were built during the early years of the nineteenth century. So, too were Brookside Cottages near the bridge. The blacksmith's shop was hereabouts and the remains of a structure to dam the stream near the ford are probably connected with it. The pub, The Horse Shoe Inn, long since demolished, was almost opposite and just below them. The school with a date stone 1842 is possibly the best indication of the size of the community in the hamlet at that time, thought to have numbered some 180 people. It is believed that there were a number of cottages within the mill boundaries that were demolished at the same time as the mill. The advent of power loom weaving had seen the rapid decline of handloom weaving and by 1851 only a few elderly weavers were left in the outlying farms of White Coppice. Rivington, by way of contrast, never had a weaving mill, though it had two spinning mills by 1797 and had a large handloom weaving population as late as 1861.

Quarrying increased enormously during the Industrial Revolution. Stronstrey Bank Quarry, (the one on the right facing the moor) was developed to produce the stone required for the building of the Goit between 1855 and 60. Earlier than that mill stones were quarried and roughly cut on the moor above the quarry. Some can still be found there today in various stages of completion. It is not known when they were quarried, nor for what purpose they were used.

Despite so many things that can only be guessed at, the picture of White Coppice as a busy industrial hamlet is clear. Its legacy today is not one of dismal decay but of a landscape greatly enhanced by the former mill ponds used to conserve water for the processes dependent upon them.

The Coke Ovens, Broadhead Valley

Opposite: Turton and Entwistle
Reservoir

Part Two

WALKS

INTRODUCTION

Terrain of this sort lends itself to recreational walking and its use over the years has produced a network of footpaths as well as the old farm and mine tracks. Many footpaths marked on the maps have disappeared, mainly through lack of use; some have been closed by building; some wired up by farmers; some have been afforested; some have become so overgrown with rushes that they can no longer be walked. The showing of a path on the map is no guarantee that it is still there. Equally other paths, particularly round the urban fringe, have been 'improved' and are no longer attractive. Local authorities have signposted quite a number of tracks where they leave the road, but this is no guarantee that the path continues, that it is easy to follow, or that it goes anywhere worthwhile. Conversely, some good paths and walks are not marked at all. This book collects together the most interesting walks, and in the notes that follow each walk, gives some account of the natural history, geology, archaeology and architectural features seen on that walk as they are relevant. Once some experience has been gained, it is easy to extend or alter the walks described, but it should be remembered that many footpaths are not sufficiently used to be easily followed and care is needed in walking them to avoid trespass. Unless otherwise stated, all paths used in the book are either rights of way or go over land where there is free access. For easy reference the walks in this book are grouped into five sections:-

Section 1. Walks around Anglezarke and Rivington.
Section 2. Walks around Bolton.
Section 3. Walks around Helmshore, Haslingden and Holcombe.
Section 4. Walks around Darwen and Tockholes.
Section 5. Long walks in the area.

Road side parking should not be used if at all possible because of congestion and the problems it causes to those whose daily business rather than pleasure takes them onto the road.

The use of the new Pathfinder series 1:25,000 maps, sheets SD61/71 Bolton (North) and SD62/72 Blackburn is most strongly recommended. The first covers Sections 1 and 2 and both are needed to cover Sections 3 and 4.

The 1:25,000 maps show the position of the museums, some ancient monuments and listed buildings, and enables the Conservation Areas to be located. The place names used in the text are as used on this map except where local tradition has used other names. Then these are given as well.

Boots are recommended for all moorland walks, but a great many of the others are suitable for shoes especially in summer. The times given are for people accustomed to walking. Family parties will need longer, good walkers less time. The times given do not allow a lot of time for stopping and looking around. Whilst most of the walks have been chosen as circular tours, some of the best are 'point to point' walks for which local bus services are useful. Ring Manchester (226) 8181, Blackburn 51112, or Rossendale 217777 for details of Corporation bus times in the various sections. Ribble also runs bus services through the Area. Their local offices: Blackburn 51234, Burnley 23125, Bolton 21021, Chorley 62247 will supply bus times. The West Pennine Moors Management Committee have produced a free leaflet setting out in great detail all the public transport services within the Area. It is available at Great House Barn Information Centre, Rivington.

In bad weather, and especially in winter, care should be exercised on the remoter moorland walks. Unless you are an experienced hill walker with a knowledge of map and compass it is better to keep to the well marked paths unless conditions are good. An anorak and over-trousers will help keep out wind and rain, and a spare sweater is always useful. In winter, woollen gloves and something to keep your ears warm, like a balaclava, are necessary. A torch and spare bar of chocolate are useful accessories in winter, too - in case you are caught by the short winter days!

If you come by car it is a good idea to have a simple change of clothing in the car. After a wet day it can make the drive home much more comfortable.

On summer evenings beware of the midges in some of the quarries such as Lester Mill - they are positively ferocious!

Finally, as the County Council is administering the Area with conservation strongly in mind, be conservation minded yourself. Do nothing that will injure your environment. Do nothing that will inter-fere with other people's enjoyment of the countryside, and do nothing that will hinder the efforts of the people who make a living from the land you enjoy visiting. To be more specific:-

1.   Take all your litter home with you.
2.   When picnicking use a gas stove, not a fire.
3.   Be careful with your matches and cigarettes. Remember the

devastating fires on the moors in the summer of 1980. Their effects can still be seen.

4. Enjoy the flowers and trees where they are growing.
5. Remember that most streams run into the reservoirs for drinking water and take care not to pollute them.
6. Close all gates so that animals cannot stray onto the road.
7. In lambing time keep your dog on a lead. A sheep in lamb that is chased by a dog and not even touched by it is liable to lose that lamb.
8. Take care not to block farm gates and access roads when you park. If at all possible use the recommmended parking places for these walks.
9. Wherever possible use stiles to cross walls and fences.

Whilst this book is primarily a guide to the excellent walking in the Area, there are many other recreational possibilities. Of a less strenuous nature are visits to the local museums, mentioned in Part One, each depicting in its own special way, life as it was lived or worked in times past. Including these museums, there are eleven ancient monuments, a number of Conservation Areas and a wealth of listed buildings.

In addition there are a large number of club-orientated leisure pursuits. Many of the reservoirs have their fishing rights let out to local angling clubs. Hang-gliding is carried out in suitable weather from Winter Hill. Though there are not many bridleways in the Area, some riding is done around Rivington. Sailing is carried on on the Belmont, Delph, and Jumbles reservoirs, and there is canoeing on the Blue Lagoon at Belmont. Rock climbing is practised at Cadshaw and many of the quarries. Orienteering and cross country runs take place in the moorland parts and there is an annual race up Rivington Pike and a race around the Three Towers. As yet water ski-ing and skin diving are not permitted in the reservoirs, but it is evident that, leaving aside the wide fields for ornithological and botanical studies, there is a wealth of leisure opportunity in the Area.

1. WALKS AROUND RIVINGTON, ANGLEZARKE AND WHITE COPPICE

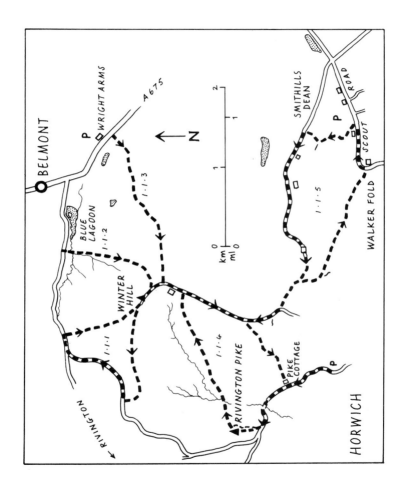

THE ASCENT OF WINTER HILL   WALK NO.1.1

Ascent is rather a grand word to use for a mere hill, but at a height of 1,498 feet, or 456 metres, Winter Hill is the highest point in the West Pennine Moors Area. There are several ways of making the ascent. Best are:-

1.   From the highest point of the Rivington-Belmont road. This is short and sharp.

Time: 30mins. to the top, 1hr-1hr. 30mins. for the circuit.

2.   From above the Blue Lagoon (Wards Reservoir on the O.S. map), Belmont.

Time: about 30mins. to the top. Possibly the best ascent of all. It is direct and fairly dry.

3.   From Belmont. This is the nicest way on a fine morning and best for shoes.

Time: 1hr. to the top, 2hrs. for the circuit.

4.   From Rivington Pike. Have boots or wellies or wet feet.

Time: ¾hr. from the Pike or 1hr. 35mins. from the road end for the round walk.

5.   From the Scout Road. Longest in distance, but a gentle ascent easy to follow.

Time: 1hr. to the top, 2hrs. for the circuit.

1.   From the top of the Rivington-Belmont Road

There's room to park there. The track runs direct from the road by the wall to the masts. It's pretty wet in parts and disappears just as you need it most, that's to say, when it gets steep. Just engage bottom gear and grunt slowly on. The Ordnance Survey cairn is just to the left, before you get to the masts. If visibility is good, the view can be very wide - see Walk No.1.3 for a description of the views to the west. To the north Great Hill is only a couple of miles away; beyond it the Bowland Fells stand clear. Further right, Pendle, Penyghent, Ingleborough and Whernside can be seen occasionally. Darwen Tower is unmistakable and always on view, but industrial haze often hides Holcombe Tower, the other one of the three hill top towers in the Area. It's a fine moorland walk to visit all three in the day. (See Walk No.5.1) Between Darwen and Holcombe Towers is featureless moorland, difficult to identify unless there's fog in the valleys and the tops are clear, a rare state of affairs occuring only in winter.

Instead of returning as you came, it makes a pleasant extension of the walk to go along the edge of the moor towards the sea. A little track starts just past the masts and runs to the tumulus that can be

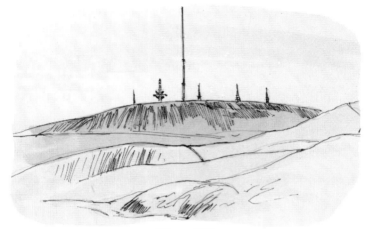

Winter Hill

seen as a pip on the moor. When you come to the boggy hollow (full of cotton grass in June), bear left a little and find the driest way you can. At the tumulus you will see the rough road that runs round the Pike about 100 yards away. Turn right on it and a further 20 minutes will see you back to your car.

2. From the Blue Lagoon

Cross the little stream and make for the obvious stile above. Now just follow the well trodden path to the near end of Winter Hill. The O.S. trig point is a little further along. Return by Walk 1.1, or if you prefer, go down the track to the Wright Arms. To find it, simply follow the tarmac road to the first corner and pick it up there. Return from the Wright Arms is, however, along the road.

3. From Belmont village

Convenient parking is a bit of a problem. The track starts almost opposite the Wright Arms, ½mile on the Bolton side of the village. There's parking there for customers, so maybe you first fortify yourself and later refresh yourself! Otherwise find a back street or go up to the Blue Lagoon on the Rivington road. There, at least, it is convenient for the return if you do the circular walk.

From the pub, cross the road, and take the track that starts in the corner of the fir plantation. It goes right through it and then slants to

The Blue Lagoon, Belmont

the right, climbing gently all the way to the top. There's a garden seat about three quarters of the way up if you're flagging. Once on the tarmac at the top, turn right and go boldly on through the gate and look for the cairn on the right before you pass the masts. Either retrace your steps or descend the steep slope overlooking the road. it's best to go a good 100 yards further on than the cairn before descending. Take care on this. If you fall, you're liable to roll or slide - unpleasant. Once on the road, turn right and follow it back to Belmont.

4. From Rivington Pike

To get the best out of this walk, go on a sunny evening in a dry spell, otherwise, unless you've got good boots, you'll get very wet feet. If you want the shortest possible approach to the Pike, turn up Georges Lane, Horwich. It leaves the B6226 almost opposite the Jolly Crofters, becomes very rough but is motorable. You can stop just below the Pike which is about 10 minutes walk, best approached from the right. It is a splendid viewpoint on a clear evening.

From the top of the Pike a broad squelchy track leads straight to the T.V. mast. It will take longer than you think, and when you reach the road made of railway sleepers cross it and continue to the tarmac road. Follow this past the T.V. station and the Scotsman's Stump. Where the road ends by the police radio masts, go boldly on, and you will find the cairn on the right before you've passed the masts. Now follow the little path to the tumulus (see Route No.1) and there keep straight on down (steep) to the rough road. Turn left on this, and about 20mins. will see you back at your car. If you don't care to drive that extremely rough road, park where the tarmac ends and walk along it instead. Then it is better to return as follows: From the T.V. station follow the tarmac road down towards Horwich until it starts to bend to the left and you can see a big stone cairn straight ahead. You will see a broad but rather faint track going off to the right. Follow this down to Pike Cottage, turn left, and a few minutes sees you back.

5. From the Scout Road

The Scout Road is the narrow moorland road joining the B6226 at the Bob Smithy Inn with the A675 near the Wilton Arms. Smithills Dean Road joins the Scout Road at about half way. Across from Smithills Dean Road is an unclassified road which can be used to start the walk. With a car, however, if the circular walk is to be undertaken it is better to park at Colliers Row, near Brownstones Quarry, about a half mile west of the crossroads.

Follow the unmade road by the side of the cottages, pass the farm and turn right. Turn left on the tarmac road. The house on the left below the road was the inspiration for *Grimsdyke*, a children's novel by Walt Unsworth, set in these moors (though the actual site was Hempshaw's on the Anglezarke Moor). Where the road forks keep to the right. After a bit a stile is crossed and the road becomes a path. Quite distinct and easy to follow to the masts.

To return, go down the road from the masts until a track is seen on the left leading down into Dean Brook, the broad valley on the left. Good at first the path is hard to follow in the middle but soon recovers and becomes a good bridle path leading to Walker Fold. Turn left up the road and five minutes walk brings you back to Colliers Row.

Notes about Winter Hill

Winter Hill owes it steep northern slope to faulting and subsequent weathering of the fault. All of Winter Hill is typical moorland containing many boggy places. Cotton grass grows in the wettest places, an indication to avoid them if you can. One relatively rare and interesting plant of the wet places is the cranberry. There's a big patch of it on top, but I'll not tell you just where. In any case, it produces far too few berries to make any luscious cranberry sauce.

Winter Hill has been the scene of man's handiwork since prehistoric times. There is a neolithic burial mound about ¼ mile west of the cairn, but today it has practically disappeared. It is thought to date to 1500 B.C. Of greater interest to archaeologists is the tumulus that I described as a 'pip on the moor'. This is the Noon Hill Ring Cairn. It has been excavated and a shattered burial urn was recovered and has been restored and placed in Bolton Municipal Museum.

Much later, coal was mined and the remains of old coal pits can be seen here and there. There is one, now fenced round, near the road by the Post Office mast, and there are many others. They were worked in the late 18th and early 19th centuries, and are known as 'bell pits'. On the moors the coal seams are close to the surface and the winning of coal did not present the technical problems that deeper though more readily accessible pits would have done.

The Scotsman's Stump is a memorial to one James Henderson, a native of Annan, Dumfriesshire, who was brutally murdered on Nov. 9th 1803, on Rivington Moor.* He was a pedlar, travelling from Wigan or Blackrod to Belmont and Blackburn. At that time this was the most direct road between those places.

Later still came technological man. The police masts near the O.S. cairn were the first of all the masts to be built in 1948, then followed the first T.V. mast in 1955, soon to be replaced by the present tubular mast which is over 1,000ft. (328 metres) high. The P.O. mast was built in 1955. Truly, man has made use of these moors!

THE ASCENT OF RIVINGTON PIKE   WALK NO.1.2

Judging by the amount of footpath erosion on it, Rivington Pike must be the most popular hill in the whole of the West Pennine Moors, and with some justification. It is easy of access, is dry under foot and an extremely fine viewpoint. It can very easily be incorporated into a visit to the Terrace Gardens, (see Walk No.1.3) but as an enjoyable ascent it is best done from the car park known as Old Kate's Dingle. To find this from Rivington, go up the Belmont road, narrow and tricky if there is much traffic, turn right at the T-junction and keep straight on at the next junction. It is signed as 'no through road' and there is a fair amount of space at the end for parking but it is very popular at weekends.

From the upper end of the car park follow the right-hand one of two rough roads until you have crossed a deep cut ravine. Then on the left there is a pair of stiles and a well made path takes you to the edge of the Terrace Gardens at a fairly high level. Go upwards towards the Dove Cote and when you reach the terrace where there is a large pond - possibly dry in summer - turn right and follow this level or a higher one where there is a choice until you emerge from the gardens at the

* Recent research suggests he was accidentally shot by a shooting party on the moor.

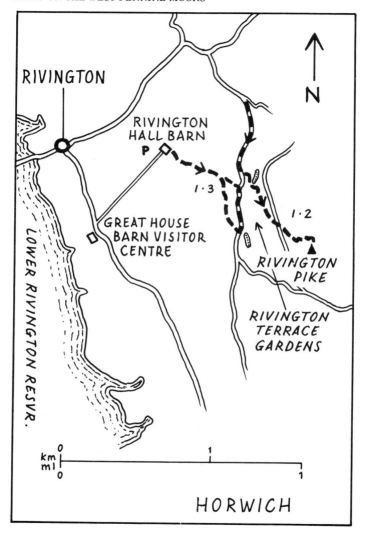

RIVINGTON

RIVINGTON
HALL BARN
P

1·3

GREAT HOUSE
BARN VISITOR
CENTRE

1·2

RIVINGTON
PIKE

LOWER RIVINGTON RESVR.

RIVINGTON
TERRACE
GARDENS

N

km 0
ml 0
1
1

HORWICH

south end. The Pike then lies straight ahead, and is reached by an obvious path. Avoid the badly eroded front: there is a much better and easier path round the back.

For your return it is best to go well to the right and to drop a little to find the terrace where the great staircase ends close to the pond. Then go down this to its end just below the rough road, turn right to gain this and then follow it down to the car park again. If you want to visit the Hall Barn on your way back, cross the first stile on your left after you've passed the ravine, turn right on the cinder track below and follow it round to find the Barn in about 5 minutes. To find the return, see Walk No.1.4.4.

Notes about Rivington Pike

Rivington Pike, 1,198ft. or 365 metres high, is known to have been the site of an ancient beacon, one of a chain of signal fires used to send warnings in time of danger. It is said to have been in use by 1138 A.D., and there is a written record that it was lit on July 1st 1588, when the Armada was sailing up the Channel. The Tower was built in 1733 on the beacon platform, using some of the stones. Originally it had a roof, doors and windows, and was used as a shooting lodge at one time. It fell into disrepair and was wilfully damaged, but it has now been restored. It is a Grade 2 listed building.

The Pike is the best place for late evening and sunset views in the whole Area. Go there some clear summer evening, preferably a Saturday when there is less industrial smoke, and contrive to be on the Pike about an hour before sunset. Then, if you have a bit of luck, the evening sky will be bright, the sea will be lit up, and the hills of North Wales and the Lake District will be silhouetted against the sea, giving the best possible conditions of long distance viewing. See the previous Walk for instructions on how to get to the Pike quickly.

Having got there, what can you expect to see? As far left as possible, where the view is cut off by Rivington Moor, you can just make out the outline of the Staffordshire Hills, but the first bold one on the left is HELSBY HILL, 35 miles away, and seen right behind the cooling towers of the power station at Fiddlers Ferry. Slightly to its right stands the long undulating range of the CLWYDIAN HILLS which separate Mold and Denbigh. They are 45 miles away and you can see them quite often. To their right, between the nearby Harrock Hill and Ashurst Beacon (you can see the beacon through binoculars), is Snowdonia itself, or more precisely, the CARNEDDAU. They apparently end where GT. ORME dips into the sea. This is 60 miles away. Even further to the right, a full 80 miles away, and only seen if

Rivington Pike from the path to Winter Hill

conditions are really good, is the tip of ANGLESEY. Sometimes, if the sea is well lighted, you can see the whole of the coast-line of Liverpool Bay.

Coming much nearer home is the gasometer at Southport, then you can see the Ribble and its tributary that rises on Winter Hill, the Douglas. Then follows BLACKPOOL TOWER and the elevators at Fleetwood. Across Morecambe Bay is the whaleback of BLACK

COMBE, most westerly of the Lakeland Hills and quite often seen. It's 55 miles away. A mass of undulating high ground separates it from the next distinctive pair of hills, DOW CRAG and CONISTON OLD MAN, and at the other end of that block of rather higher ground, you can see the shoulder of BOWFELL dipping in to Langdale. The LANGDALE PIKES themselves can only just be seen, they're so small, but the drop to Dunmail Raise and the climb to HELVELLYN is visible. Then the nearer BOWLANDS cut off any further views to the right. It's a truly wonderful panorama.

These long distance views will very likely make you ask, 'Why couldn't I see the Isle of Man'? and, 'Just how far can I see when it's really clear'? It's very difficult to answer these questions simply. The distance depends very much on how clear 'really clear' is. Moisture is always present in our atmosphere to some extent, and it is never as clear here as in the Alps or Himalaya. There are five other important points:-

1. The height you are above sea level.
2. The height of the mountain or other object you are looking at.
3. The curvature of the earth.
4. Refraction.
5. The difference in brightness between the object you are looking at and its background, and, obviously, its size.

If you are 1,000ft. above sea level then you can see the horizon at sea level 41.83 miles away. At 2,000ft. this increases to 59.20 miles. Obviously if you're looking at high mountains like Snowdonia you will be able to see them further away than the horizon itself. The thing whose effect is difficult to calculate is refraction. Refraction is the bending of rays of light around the earth and has the effect of enabling you to see round the curvature of the earth, as it were, and observe even more distant objects. An extreme case is the mirage in the desert. As the effect of refraction depends upon the temperature of the air, you can see how difficult it is to estimate its effect. The difference in brightness or optical contrast doesn't so much affect the distance you can see, but rather whether or not your eye can pick out the object you're looking for. It's much the same thing in the long run.

This was demonstrated quite strikingly one day when I was returning to Hayfield from a walk over Kinder Scout. It was a dull day, and though the moorlands were clear we could not see the T.V. mast to identify Winter Hill with certainty. Then a patch of bright sky appeared in the west and rapidly spread. Suddenly we could see the mast, sharp and clear as a giant needle silhouetted against the bright sky.

In theory it should be possible to see Snowdon standing above the Carneddau, as it is 300ft. higher than them. In practice the light is always too uniform and 300ft. is barely sufficient to see at that distance. It ought to be possible to see the Isle of Man, though at 95 miles distant it is considerably more than any of the hills listed. I have never seen it despite many good clear evenings on the Pike. I have, however, seen St. Bees head, the most westerly point of Cumbria, from North Wales, and that is an incredible 110 miles away, but Rivington Pike was too small to be seen and was lost against the background of the moors. St. Bees juts out into the sea and was clear and unmistakable. It seems that we need unusual conditions of the atmosphere to see the Isle of Man.

Now if you have a half inch or similar Merseyside map, just have a look at it. You will see that a line drawn on the map from the Pike to the Menai Straits shows that the Straits cannot be seen as a clear gap between the mainland and the island of Anglesey. Yet you could see a very large gap indeed, perfectly clearly. This is because the sea is forming the horizon considerably closer than the Menai Straits, and Anglesey and Snowdonia are seen further away partly because they are higher and partly because of refraction.

TWO WALKS ROUND RIVINGTON TERRACE GARDENS
WALK NO.1.3

These gardens, part of Viscount Leverhulme's Rivington estate, were planned on a vast scale along the steep hillside with the aid of a landscape architect, Mr. T.H.Mawson. They took almost twenty years to build, indeed, work was still going on at Leverhulme's death in 1925. Thousands of trees and shrubs of many varieties were planted. Only those with a robust constitution have survived, though the knowledgeable gardener may spot some rare ones tucked away, for example a double rhododendron near the Great Lawn.

A very rough public road runs diagonally through the gardens, climbing up from Horwich to where there was once an entrance, and then dropping to meet the Rivington-Belmont road. The two parts are linked by an elegant stone footbridge.

You don't need detailed instructions to enjoy these gardens. It is one of their special pleasures to find out what lies round the next corner or up the next flight of steps, but it is worth knowing that a toilet block has been built at the very top, just below the Pike.

You can easily spend a whole afternoon wandering around, and then

The Dove Cote and Ornamental Gardens

you may not have seen everything. It's a place that repays many visits. It is probably best to park at Rivington Hall Barn to explore the lower part. To find this take the Rivington road from Horwich just below the roundabout at the junction of the B6226 and the A675. At Great House Barn Visitor Centre, take the avenue on the right straight to Rivington Hall and Barn.

Leave the car park behind the barn, keep to the right of the cottage and take the lane that winds up the hill. In about 100 yards you will come in sight of an open meadow with swing gate. Go through this, follow the path up the field to the next stile and enter the woods of the Bungalow Gardens, yet another name for them. Do not be in a hurry to climb upward and you will come to the start of one of several magnificent stone staircases climbing the hillside. Close by is a deep cut 'fairy dell' with man-made pools, waterfalls and grottoes. Work your way upwards to the rough road that divides the gardens, and turn

57

left on it until you come to the footbridge. Here, a very steep narrow set of steps not a staircase will bring you back to the bottom, but in between are many level paved paths and other sets of steps that give enjoyable wandering.

You can best visit the upper and more interesting part by parking at the end of the short metalled road that branches off the Rivington-Belmont road just below Moses Cocker Farm (parking difficult at weekends). Walk along this road to the bridge mentioned above, and enter the gardens by the splendid staircase that starts from it. Originally, of course, there was no access from this road, but the passage of many feet has worn a clear track to its lower end. Take the climb slowly. Enjoy the view from the arbours so conveniently built for this purpose. High on the left is the tower that was originally a dovecote. Below, to its right, is a fish pond at one time fed by a spring cascading down the hill. Away to the right is a pergola where there was a rose garden, and below it, across one of the main access roads to the Bungalow, the remains of the kitchen gardens, still partly walled for shelter, yet in the sun. Below these and further right still are the poor remains of the once exotic Oriental Garden. Gone are the pagoda-like buildings and the footbridge that created a scene reminiscent of that on a willow pattern plate.

The Bungalow itself, the heart of the fine gardens, where was that? It was built quite high up, not far below the Pike. The original one was a timber and tile affair, the very essence of a bungalow in appearance, and it was burnt down by Suffragettes on 7th July 1913. This was ironical, as Viscount Leverhulme was not unsympathetic to their cause. However, without delay he had the site cleared and built a very substantial 'Ye Olde' type bungalow in stone. It was L shaped and stood on the top of a pair of lawns, the lower one enclosed by the corner of the L. A fine quadrant shaped flight of stairs still stands in this corner connecting the two lawns and will help you to identify the place. On the top lawn a few coloured tiles are all that remain of that once palatial bungalow. What happened to it?

It's a sad story indeed, and coupled with the neglect of the once wonderful gardens, an even sadder comment on the value we placed on our environment in 1945-50. Admittedly, there were more pressing problems then. When Viscount Leverhulme died, the estates were sold to a Mr. Magee of Bolton, and on his death to Liverpool Corporation. It would seem likely that they bought them in order to consolidate their position as principal landowner with an especial responsibility for the purity of the water they supplied. They must have found the Bungalow something of a white elephant and expensive to maintain. A conference of local authorities called in 1947 to discuss possible uses of the Bungalow failed to agree to any solution, and the Corporation subsequently demolished it and allowed the gardens to be despoiled. By 1970 or thereabouts, the climate of public opinion had changed and in 1974 the North West Water Authority, who now owned the Terraced Gardens, started to open up the paths and restore the decaying stonework. Rhododendrons and sapling trees had made such vigorous growth that the place was a veritable jungle, penetrable only by small boys creeping Red Indian fashion along tunnels in the undergrowth.

Now the major terraces and connecting steps and staircases have been cleared of overhanging trees and shrubs. Many staircases, arbours, and the pergola have been truly restored in matching stonework. Some archways and flights of stairs have been excavated from accumulated debris, and in 1976 the Dovecote, a Grade 2 listed building, was re-roofed. Two ponds have been excavated but do not at present, seem to be holding water too well. All this work, much of it real hard graft, has been carried out by parties of volunteers working under the supervision of the National Conservation Corps and the British Trust for Conservation who were given a grant by the N.W.W.A. in 1975. Their efforts, which are still continuing, have now made the gardens a splendid place in which to wander at all times of the year. We can only marvel at the sort of place it once was for it is clearly not practicable to restore them fully. A collection of old photographs in Chorley Reference Library give just an inkling of the place in its pomp and glory.

Those who want to know more about the bungalow and gardens should read *Leverhulme's Rivington*, by M.J.Smith and published privately. Alternatively the Visitor Centre sells a leaflet for only 15p that gives a great deal of information and takes you round a waymarked trail, but be warned, the waymarkers are often removed or twisted round.

STROLLS AROUND LEVER PARK   WALK NO.1.4

Lever Park is no extension of a town park but a great chunk of varied and open countryside, once part of Lord Leverhulme's Rivington Estates, and still bearing signs of his handiwork. Today it has been designated a country park. You can find it very easily from Horwich, taking the road to Rivington which leaves the A673 just below the roundabout near the Crown Hotel. About a mile and a half along that road you will come to the Great House Barn Visitor and Information Centre. Its car park is primarily for visitors to the Centre and it is for short stays only, but it may be used for the hour or so that it will take you to do the first two of these strolls. If this car park is full return to Middle Derbyshires car park and picnic area which is almost opposite the large secondary school. It is equally convenient for the first walk. All the walks in Lever Park are suitable for shoes and any weather.

ALONG THE RESERVOIR BANK TO RIVINGTON CASTLE
WALK NO.1.4.1

Time: about an hour. Best in early spring when the sun can be seen glinting on the water through the leafless trees.

Walk towards the reservoir through the childrens' playground and you will find a well made path just inside the fence. Turn left and follow it very pleasantly to the Castle, an imitation ruin. There is no admittance to it because it is unsafe, but at some future date it will be restored and there will be admittance. Three tree-lined avenues converge on it. Take the right-hand one to a crossroads of wide paths. Take the right-hand one again and follow it to the Middle Derbyshires car park (portaloos). From its left-hand end near the road a well made path leads unmistakably through Lever Park to the road within a very short distance of the Visitor Centre.

TO RIVINGTON, RETURNING BY THE RESERVOIR BANK
WALK NO.1.4.2

Time: about 30-40 minutes.

A new footpath has been made to the village leaving the car park at its entrance. Just turn left and follow it. You will find the post office, built in 1810 on the village green and just beyond is the Unitarian Chapel, well worth a look inside. Turn left at the road junction. On your right perched on a knoll and hidden by trees is the church, usually locked, and on your left, the village school. Immediately beyond the school turn left into a wide gravel track, a road almost, and follow it back to the Visitor Centre.

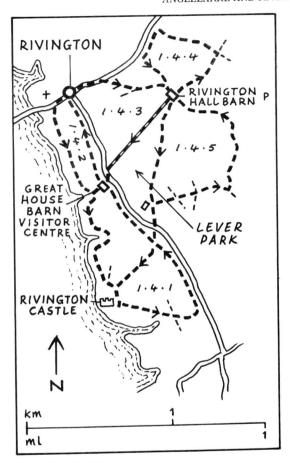

Walks From The Hall Barn
TO THE VISITOR CENTRE AND THE VILLAGE

WALK NO.1.4.3

To find the car park at the Hall Barn, drive up the fine avenue opposite the Visitor Centre and bear left before you get to the iron railings of the Hall. There is a much larger car parking area here than

61

at the Visitor Centre as well as refreshments. There are toilets next to the Visitor Centre.

Time for this walk, about 1 hour.

Whether you need refreshments or not, first have a look at the interior of this remarkable building and see the notes at the end of this chapter for something about it. Then go in front of the Hall onto the avenue that leads to the Visitor Centre. At the Centre turn right onto the footpath that leads to Rivington Village and at the village green turn right onto the Belmont road. Turn right immediately behind the last house and go through the left-hand one of the two stiles opposite. Follow first a grassy cart track then a wide tree-lined road back to the Hall Barn.

FIELD PATHS ROUND THE HALL BARN   WALK NO.1.4.4

Time: a short hour. The route is waymarked through the fields but is little trodden and very attractive though there are some muddy stretches in wet weather.

Leave the car park by the cart track at the back of the barn and turn left at once in front of the cottages. When you reach the rough road at the top of the wood turn left and keep going straight ahead to a swing gate from where there are good views over Chorley. Go straight down the field to a wide gap in the wall, then bearing left a little make for the middle of the next wall. Turn right and follow it to the road. Here you will find a pleasant footpath through trees, turn left and follow it to a stile just above the first house. Turn left here and follow first a grassy cart track then a wide rough tree-lined track back to the Hall Barn.

THE LOWER WOODS OF THE TERRACE GARDENS
WALK NO.1.4.5

There are many rough roads and tree-lined avenues in Lever Park that give acceptable walking but because they are straight, soon become boring. This walk uses one that winds around and is much more enjoyable. There are good views on a fine winter's day when there are no leaves on the trees.

Time: about 1 hour.

Wherever you are parked in this large car park make for the Hall Barn in order to get started correctly. Turn right at the front of the Barn and left as soon as you have passed the iron railings in front of the Hall. You are now on a wide cart track. Go straight ahead at the 'crossroads' and when you reach a farm on your right after about 20 minutes turn left through a swing gate. Go straight across two tree-lined avenues and through another swing gate into the base of the wood. A broad path climbs steadily to the right, but you follow it only a short distance, as far as the path that leaves it on the left, which you now take. Cross the bridge and follow the path along the hillside until it ends abruptly at a flight of steep steps. Go up these, they are quite short, and you will find yourself in front of an ornate garden shelter. Turn left and follow the path down to the Hall Barn. There are fine views of the Yarrow and Anglezarke reservoirs.

A GRAND TOUR OF LEVER PARK   WALK NO.**1.4.6**

Parts of these walks can be combined to give a good circuit of the Park lasting about 2 hours.

From the Hall Barn car park start by Walk 1.4.5 and go as far as the farm where you keep straight on to the road. Cross it onto a path that takes you to a house in the trees. Turn left here and you are on the central one of the three avenues that lead to Rivington Castle. At the Castle turn right and reverse Walk 1.4.1 to the Visitor Centre, then to the Hall Barn by Walk 1.4.2 and reversing Walk 1.4.3.

Notes about Lever Park and the buildings in it.
A pair of granite pillars mark the entrance to Lever Park Avenue, Horwich, the left-hand one of which bears the following inscription:

LEVER PARK
THE GIFT OF
WILLIAM HESKETH LEVER
1st VISCOUNT LEVERHULME
BORN AT 6 WOOD STREET BOLTON
SEPTEMBER 19th 1861
DIED AT HAMPSTEAD LONDON
MAY 7th 1925
FOR THE BENEFIT OF THE CITIZENS
OF HIS NATIVE TOWN AND NEIGHBOURHOOD
BY ACT OF PARLIAMENT IN 1902 THE
OWNERSHIP AND CARE OF THE PARK
WERE VESTED IN THE
CORPORATION OF THE CITY OF LIVERPOOL

This, in a nutshell, is the story of Lever Park, the Rivington Bungalow, and the Ornamental Gardens. Mr. W.H.Lever amassed a huge fortune in producing a soap that was far better than any available at the time. It was known as Sunlight Soap, a household word even today. His chemist's skill in formulating the soap and his own business acumen laid the foundation of a company that eventually became the world-wide Unilever.

Before Mr. Lever, as he was then, bought the Rivington Estates all this area was good farmed land divided into small fields. Most of it was pasture, a little was arable. Now most of it has not been farmed for some 80 years and it is reverting to nature. Scrub birch and oak trees have seeded themselves freely, coarse grass and rushes have taken over the former good pastures. Farming's loss is wildlife's gain, for scrub woodland, particularly oak woodland, is a good habitat for many small birds.

He bought Rivington Hall and manor in 1900. The Estate included land which is now known as Lever Park. At once he started to indulge in his passion for fresh air and gardens, building the Bungalow and the Ornamental Terrace Gardens below the Pike. He acquired a collection of animals such as fallow deer, zebu, emus and wallabies, and kept them in the park in the open air behind stout iron fences, a number of which remain. In 1901 Mr. Lever most generously attempted to give a large part of his estates to the citizens of Bolton, but because of legal wrangles with Liverpool Corporation, the procedure noted on the pillar was required.

The Terrace Gardens, though open to the public today (see Walk No.1.3) were not part of the original gift of land. The Pike, however, was included in the original gift, and included land above the 1,250ft. contour, and wide access to if from the high road. This must surely have been one of the earliest gifts of hill country ever made to the people of the British Isles. Shortly afterwards Mr. Lever became 1st Viscount Leverhulme.

Rivington Castle with its three approaches of tree-lined avenues was perhaps Viscount Leverhulme's only 'folly'. Eccentric he may have been, generous to a degree, and even this replica of Liverpool Castle, a ruin on Liverpool Bay, was an idea for the benefit of the public that was never completed. There should have been a terrace café, set in rose gardens, overlooking the lake. How delightful that would have been today!

Rivington is quite an ancient village. It lost its pub but little else when the Lower Rivington Reservoir was built. The school, now only for juniors, was founded in 1566 by Bishop Pilkington, third son of Richard Pilkington of Rivington Hall. The present building dates from 1714 and is on the original site. The Church has no special features and has been re-built a number of times. The Unitarian Chapel, a rather austere building, is one of the earliest in Lancashire,

Cruick built barn, Rivington Information Centre

dating back to 1703. There are stones bearing considerably earlier dates in its graveyard. The present Rivington Hall is a late Georgian building replacing in 1780 an earlier Tudor structure, and it is thought that in Saxon times there was a manor there.

The Hall Barn is a most unusual building. It is what is known as a cruick built, using massive split oak trees standing on low stone pillars to support the roof. This method of construction was used from Saxon times until the end of the eighteenth century, or even later where good timber was available. A precise date cannot be given to the Hall Barn from the available information, but it is thought to have been built about 1550, a period of agricultural prosperity in rural England, when the wealth of the monasteries, dissolved in 1536, had been distributed around the countryside and the skills of monastic craftsmen were still available. The Barn was still used as such when Lord Leverhulme bought the Hall Estate. He 'restored' it between 1900 and 1910 adding the two side aisles and the porch and re-roofing it. The original roof was almost certainly heather. This was virtually a conversion to a mock Tudor dance hall-cum-tea room, a travesty of restoration as it is carried out today. Great House Barn, known locally as the Little Barn has a similar construction and was restored at the same time. The Little Barn has only two pairs of cruicks or roof trusses, instead of six in

65

the Hall Barn, it is much smaller and is thought to be older than the Hall Barn. The Hall Barn is over 100ft. long, 57ft wide and almost 25ft at the point of the roof. Both the Hall Barn and Great House Barn are Grade 1 listed buildings. The Hall, Castle, Church and Chapel are Grade 2 listed buildings. The school is Grade 2B.

Under the plan for recreation in the West Pennine Moors Area, Lever Park will be designated a Country Park, and at some future date will be extended to include the Pike and the moor behind as far as Winter Hill.

A WALK ROUND THREE ARCHAEOLOGICAL SITES
AT RIVINGTON
WALK NO.1.5

It is an unfortunate fact that many archaeological remains in the Area have been buried, destroyed or otherwise lost. In the case of the Twa Lads burial mounds on Wilders Moor and the tumulus on Winter Hill little remains except heaps of stones and patches of a different kind of vegetation. The remains at Noon Hill Slack, an oulier of Winter Hill, fortunately give something worth looking at.

The best approach is to drive up Georges Lane, Horwich, which starts opposite the Jolly Crofters on the B6226, just south of Horwich. After a lot of potholes the metalled section ends. It's easy to park there.

Time: 1½-2 hours.

Continue along the rough road to Pike Cottage and there take the footpath that goes up the moor. It keeps left of the true top of the Twa Lads Moor, but make a diversion to the top when it is within easy reach. The big cairn is a modern structure, and though the site is said to have been an Iron Age fort there is no evidence left today. The Twa Lads cairns were not here but on the flank of the hill above the path. When the first edition of this book was written they could be identified, but no longer.

Return to the path and follow it to the tarmac road leading to the T.V. station. Go diagonally left at the end of the station buildings, aiming for the P.O. mast. There is a little path that cuts the corner and passes some of the old coal pits which abound on Winter Hill. Go through the gate across the road, pass the police masts and continue on a well marked path that slopes gently down to Noon Hill Slack. Don't rush it. Start looking on the left, right up against the track about 300 yards from the fence for the next tumulus site. It's a patch of very green grass with a lot of stone around the edge, and it's easier

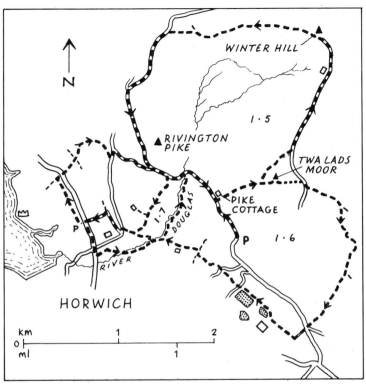

to see looking up the hill than down it. Having found it, continue along the path to Noon Hill Slack, easily seen as a pip on the moor straight ahead. Avoid the wet hollow as best you can by keeping to the left. Again follow the same little track straight ahead down to the rough road that runs around the Pike, where a left turn will take you back to your car in about 30 minutes and give you fine south-westward views all the way.

Archaeological Notes

The Twa Lads was originally a Bronze Age twin cairn - hence the name. It has not been excavated in modern times but was opened up in the seventeenth century and all evidence lost. Until fairly recently a heap of stones marked the spot. It seems likely that they have been

67

removed to build the fine cairn on top of Wilders Moor, only a short distance away. Thus is archaeological evidence lost for ever. Were it not that the site is known, and listed, it would soon be forgotten.

The tumulus just west of the summit on Winter Hill was excavated in 1958 by Manchester University and Chorley Archaeological Society, whose report is filed in Chorley Library. The mound had been opened at some time unknown and the remains removed. It was thought to date to about 1500 B.C. that is to say, Early Bronze Age. Evidently any restoration work was quite inadequate, for today little remains. Though the site yielded little of archaeological importance it was found that the turf beneath the mound was intact, and this yielded valuable information about the vegetation at that time. Cotton grass, ferns, heather and bilberry were found and pollen studies showed that oak, alder, birch and hazel trees were present locally.

The cairn on Noon Hill Slack was excavated at the same time. It is a typical Pennine Early Bronze Age burial mound dated between 2000 and 1400 B.C., very similar to the one on Winter Hill. Excavation showed it to have a curb of large stones and inside there was evidence of four burials in stone cists after cremation and one in an urn of the food vessel type. Cairns such as these were used for several burials, not necessarily at the same time. It is still quite well seen as a circle 50ft. in diameter and originally it stood 6ft. above the moor. Some collapse of the interior seems to have taken place, for it was used by local non-conformists as a meeting place in the early days of the break from the established church when it was still illegal to have a church building. Much of the excavated material has been restored and is displayed in the Bolton Municipal Museums.

TWA LADS MOOR AND BURNT EDGE   WALK NO.1.6

By way of contrast with the previous walk this one includes a fair measure of industrial archaeology. It also has very good views over the Lancashire plain.

Start from Middle Derbyshires car park. To find it see Walk No.1.4.

Time: about 3 hours. Light boots recommended.

Leave the car park by the signed path leading to Great House Barn Information Centre. When you reach a bridleway lined with young trees leading to Rivington Castle turn right on it. Go straight across the road and at the 'crossroads' of the avenues just beyond Gilsbrook again go straight across. In a few minutes you come to a gate across the ride and on its right, some 50 yards away, there is another gate and stile. Go through this and soon after through yet another gate or stile onto a wide roughly cobbled track that climbs up the edge of the wood.

Follow it round two sharp hairpin bends, (take care not to miss the first one and go straight down to Rivington School) and reach the rough road below the Pike. Turn right and continue to the solitary house, Pike Cottage, which you see as soon as you reach this road. Turn left over the stile by the cottage and follow the well trodden path that goes over the left flank of the moor. To reach the top, bear right on a less well marked track, and just aim for the large cairn from where there is a fine view over the Lancashire plain with just a little more to be seen of the Manchester area than from the Pike.

From the top you have two options. The way lies straight ahead to the wide swinging corner of the road. It is not far but the ground is very rough and wet with a large ditch to cross just before the road. If you don't fancy it aim well left to regain your track further up the flank of the moor.

Assuming you do this, at the road turn right and at the big swinging corner look for a wooden stile set well back from the road. There the track leads you into a shallow valley. Follow the track through the heather until you come to a broken dam on your right. You may not immediately recognise it for what it is, as the water behind it has long since flowed away and it is grown with rushes. Cross the stream and the dam, turn left, go over a little rise and continue down the valley until you come to a Y-junction with a public footpath fingerpost. Take the right-hand one up to the wall and follow the wall to a stile and gate side by side. Go through the gate and follow the walled track straight, truly straight, down the hill passing Pilkington's Quarry, a monstrous growling hole if work is in progress, onto the tarmac of Georges Lane. This will take a relaxing 15 minutes or so, enjoy the view as you go. Beyond the M6, Blackrod stands astride a long hillock, easily identified by its church steeple. Somewhat to the left and further away you may see Ashurst Beacon and Parbold Hill, and further still the gasometer at Southport.

Go straight across Georges Lane staying close to the wall. Almost at the bottom turn right through a little gate into a house garden - astonishing, but this is the path. Then on to the cinder road beyond. Turn right and after about 200yds. you will be opposite the former Wallsuches Bleach Works. Go up a modest flight of steps on your right. You will find yourself on the bank of a little reservoir, used to supply water to the works. Turn left and follow a well trodden path with good views passing two more small reservoirs. Go straight across the tarmac lane and pass to the right of the house. Turn right when you come to the next lane, then left in about 50yds. Pass between the houses and when you meet the next lane go right then immediately left. You are now approaching Ormston's Farm, named on the map and still (1986) a working farm. Now follow the farm access road down quite a long hill. Keep a look out for a swing gate on the right and a fenced path leading into the wood - it is easily missed. Go into the wood, cross the stream and climb the steps on the other side. Turn left at the top of them and follow the path to the stile by a gate onto a concrete farm access road. Turn left and follow it for about 100yds. until it meets two of the Rivington avenues. Turn right on the lower one and turn left at the end of the wood to reach Middle Derbyshires car park.

Things of Interest

1.   Twa Lads Moor used to have two Bronze Age burial mounds close to the track and not far from the top. In fact they gave the moor its name. They were excavated long ago and no records of their contents were ever made. Now not even their sites can be seen. The summit cairn is a modern erection and changes its shape from time to time according to the whims of passers-by.

2.   When you reach the road corner from this cairn and are walking towards the stile you may notice plenty of clinkers and cinders on the ground as well as numerous brick ends. This was the site of the boiler house of Burnt Edge Colliery and a tramway leads almost to it from the direction of the T.V. station. The ruined dam suggests that there were other early industrial works needing water power lower down the valley.

3.   If you look to the right just after you have passed Ormston Farm you will see a long narrow ridge running up the field. It is a disused tramway which brought fire clay from shallow excavations in the fields above. Nothing can be seen today, all is overgrown.

4.   Bleach and dye works were amongst the earliest factories in Lancashire. Spinning and weaving were carried out in the home before the Industrial Revolution but bleaching and dyeing were messy processes requiring vats of hot water and chemicals, not at all suited to the domestic scene. They were however, very well suited to the plentiful water supplies to be found along the Lancashire foothills. Bleach and dye works were common there in the early days of the Industrial Revolution. Knoll Wood contained one of these early bleach works. Little is left but the broken dam - well seen from the bridge over the stream - that conserved their water supply. Wallsuches was another of

these early bleach works built in 1777 for John and Thomas Ridgeway, but the buildings seen as you pass are not nearly so old as that. The great engine house has a date-stone 1854.

A WALK UP THE RIVER DOUGLAS   WALK NO.1.7

The River Douglas rises on the moor between the Pike and the post office masts and forms the south east boundary of the proposed enlarged Country Park. From just above Rivington School to the Pike its hidden valley displays a number of interesting geological features to those with a little knowledge of local geology and offers a delightful woodland walk to those who want someting 'off the beaten track'. It must be made clear that the paths are tricky and in one place potentially hazardous. Boots are strongly recommended. Allow about an hour, more if you are keen on geology. When you reach the old road beneath the Pike there are at least two alternatives for the return and their time must be added to the above.

Park at Middle Derbyshires car park.

The Route and its Points of Geological Interest

Turn right on the road, go past the private road to Blackrod and Rivington School and turn left up the next lane. When you are opposite a red brick building turn right onto a re-made footpath. Immediately you are across the bridge over the Douglas slip through a gap in the fence onto its banks. Now follow the thready path besides the stream. Leave the side of the stream at the first bend to go onto the upper bank and stay there until houses come into sight on the right. Then step down to water level again at an obvious place and go upstream a little way to the point where there are two large rounded boulders in the stream bed.

Geological Comment
You have been walking up a wide level stretch of grass, a river terrace. Terraces were formed at the end of the last Ice Age as a result of the very different level of the land with respect to the sea. The valley is quite wide at this point and the land form is easy to see. Here the rocks are soft shales and mudstones which have allowed the stream to wander about. The two large boulders in the stream bed are glacial erratics washed out of the boulder clay left by the retreating glaciers of the Ice Age.

Now keep above the stream for 50yds. or so until you come to a corner of the fence, then drop down to water level again. There's no path at first.

Geological Comment

On the right as you reach water level there is a fairly level piece of closely bedded rock that almost abuts onto one that is steeply tilted and between them is a layer of shale. This jumble of rocks is a result of a major fault across the stream that dropped the lower rocks a distance of about 250 metres.

Retrace your steps to the fence corner and follow it for 50yds. or so, well above the river which is now lost from sight in a gorge below. You should be opposite an old quarry face, not perhaps easily recognisable as such because it is quite small.

Geological Comment

The rocks of the quarry face are Ousel Nest Grit, a much harder and more massively bedded rocks than those below. These harder rocks have caused the stream to cut straight down rather than wander about. The waterfall is caused by another fault, best observed from directly above the quarry where the kink it causes in the stream is well seen.

Go down from this viewpoint to the terrace below and continue upstream easily at first then very steeply and awkwardly down to water level and continue along a steep muddy bank poised above the river for a few feet. Quite tricky at first and not for those unsure of their balance or their footing. Now the gorge disappears and you will reach a stout wooden fence. Climb over it.

Ahead lies the remains of the dam that conserved the water for the former Knoll Wood Bleach Works. Continue upstream on the same side. Half-way between the fence and the dam there is a stout sycamore tree at stream level.

Geological Comment

At its foot, almost in the water, is a band of marine shales, rich in the fossil *Gastrioceras Subcrenatum.* Though not recognisable by the untutored eye these fossils identify this shale band as a marine shale. Because it is universally present throughout the Coal Measures it enables the rocks above and below it to be identified. It lies on a bed of Rough Rock which can be seen in the stream bed above the bridge. As its name suggests, it is a coarse grained rock, often containing quartz pebbles. It was probably laid down by a stream of the Great Upper Carboniferous Delta when it was in flood. Another fault whose presence is indicated by the side stream brought it to the surface.

Return to the bridge, cross it and go right at the top of the steps. Continue along a level man-made upper platform to a broken dam.

Cross the platform and go down to the stream level again. Now continue upstream. At the end of this mound there is a stream junction and a pleasant little waterfall. Again, the cause is faulting. Go up the steps on the left of the waterfall and note the change in rock type.

Geological Comment

The massively bedded Rough Rock has been replaced by closely bedded Haslingden Flags and these continue right to the top of the wood. Climb up towards the fence, but on the level patch go right to the steam again. Here are two or three huge slabs of Haslingden Flags showing a clear ripple pattern made by a stream of that Great Upper Carboniferous Delta. Ripple patterns are very characteristic of Haslingden Flags.

Return to the main path and climb up to the fence and follow it for quite some time.

Geological Comment

Look down to the river below and note how the angle of the rock bed is the same as the angle of flow of the river itself, rather unusual, and allowing a smooth rapid flow of water.

Some 50 or 60yds. above the stone abutments of a bridge long since disappeared, the rock bed comes to an end at a little chute of water where one bank is about a foot higher than the other -more faulting.

Now make up to the path to find a stile almost at the end of the wood. You are now in pasture land and almost at once you will see a derelict stone wall on your left. It is built of Rough Rock which is lying scattered all over the field, for here you are above the Haslingden Flags. Continue up the field fairly close to the stream whose bed is made of Rough Rock.

Geological Comment

Just on the fence line are the barely distinguishable spoil heaps of two ancient coal mines, for now the strata is the Lower Sandrock Mine, a narrow coal seam worked long ago.

Go well to the left to find the stile. Climb the steep banking ahead till you reach the rough road below the Pike whose tower is clearly seen. Turn left on the road and consider your options:

A. A QUICK RETURN TO THE CAR PARK

About 50yds beyond the clump of rhododendrons there is a stile from which a well marked track leads down past Higher Knoll Farm to the road below. Turn right to find the car park.

B. ASCENT OF RIVINGTON PIKE

Bear right beyond the rhododendron patch and take the easy line to

Rivington Pike

the tower. Note the annular mound of yet another coal pit this time in the Upper Sandrock Mine, on the right as soon as you are through the gate. The top part of the Pike is however, formed of Margery Flags. From the tower go down to the near corner of the Terrace Gardens (toilets) and work your way along and down the terraces taking care to keep as near to the left-hand end of the woods as convenient. When you emerge from the woods turn left on the rough ride, go straight ahead towards Rivington Castle and keep a look out for a newly made path on the left just before the house. It will take you pleasantly back to the car park.

A WALK ROUND THE UPPER RIVINGTON AND YARROW RESERVOIRS   WALK NO.1.8

It's immaterial which way round you do this walk and it is suitable for shoes and bad weather.

Time: about 1½ hours, 2½ hours if you do the extension.

Park at the Hall Barn, Rivington. To find the Hall Barn see the instructions to Walk No.1.3.

Leave the Barn car park by a rough road on the opposite side from the Barn. It takes you to the Belmont-Rivington road where you turn left. Just below the Unitarian Chapel there is a swing gate on the right. From it a pleasant track leads to a set of steps called Forty Steps locally, though there are 41 of them. Go along the stream-side to the cinder track that leads to Deane Wood House. Follow the cinder track past Deane House and Cottage where there is a stile into the field. The path is fairly well trodden and waymarked with yellow plastic arrows right to a stile on the road. (**The extension starts here - see below**)

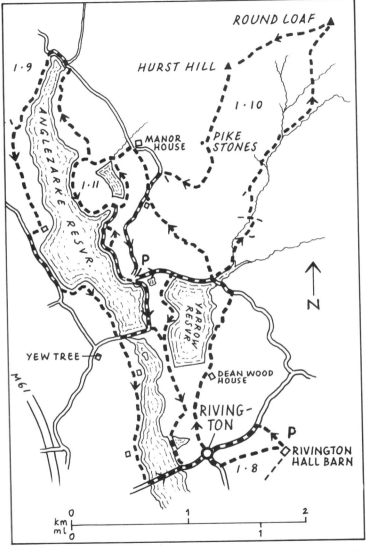

Turn left here and go down it for about ½ mile until you come to the start of a stony cart track on the left which runs below the reservoir bank. If you are only walking round the Yarrow Reservoir keep on this track all the way back to Rivington, turning right at a T-junction. It will bring you back to the village almost opposite the school and where you join the longer walk round the Lower Rivington Reservoir.

If you are walking round the Lower Rivington Reservoir as well, continue along the stony cart track only to the point where it starts to drop below reservoir level then look for a branch of it on the right. This runs down to the Anglezarke Reservoir where the overflow from the Yarrow cascades down to it. Although it only runs well in times of heavy rain, it is known as the Waterfall. Cross the dam separating the two reservoirs and turn left along the private road that runs down to the Street. It is a public footpath and gives pleasant walking through rhododendron woods. Look for a pet's grave on the right just past a third house. Later there are good views towards the Pike. When you reach the road, turn left and 5 minutes will see you in Rivington village. To find the Hall Barn car park, turn left on the first rough road after the end of the houses, or see Walk No.1.4 for other ways back.

The Extension
When you reach the road turn left and as soon as you have crossed the bridge over the arm of the reservoir continue only about another 20yds. On the right you will see a grassy cart track rising to a gate and the remains of a stile. Cross this and follow the grassy and wettish lane into the fields. Continue to follow the wall up the hill and when you reach a cross wall turn left and follow it into the next field to find a good ladder stile. As you cross the stile a fine panorama of the Lancashire plain opens out before you. You may pick out Blackpool Tower as a dark needle, and on a very good day make out the dark hump of Black Combe, a western outlier of the Lake District hills.

From the stile keep to the right of the end of the wall ahead and follow it towards the portion of fence in the wall. Cross this and make towards the right-hand end of the buildings. Go through the gate, turn left and go onto the road by the obvious and very stiff gate. Turn right on the road and after about 100yds. go over the stile on the left. Now make straight for Manor House Farm ahead. Go 20yds. further along the road and then go through the stile on the left. Follow the well trodden little path down the valley to join the path that goes round the Anglezarke Reservoir. Go straight across it and take the path that runs round the edge of the reservoir. See Walk No.1.10 for guidance. Stay on the road alongside the reservoir until you come to the outflow from the Yarrow Reservoir, a fine cascade in wet weather. Here turn left on the path that runs up through the woods and rejoins the walk by the banks of the Yarrow Reservoir. Follow this cart track to the road at the dam across the two Rivington Reservoirs, turn left and 2 minutes will see you in Rivington village.

Things of Interest Seen on These Two Walks

During the retreat of the glaciers at the end of the last Ice Age some 8 or 9 thousand years ago, the water from the melting ice formed a channel between Brinscall and Horwich. Today this is occupied by the Anglezarke and Rivington reservoirs. These three reservoirs were built in 1852-57 by Liverpool Corporation, who at the same time, took over Chorley's High Bullough Reservoir and undertook to supply Chorley with water.

The whole scheme cost £1.35M and collected water from every hill stream in the entire valley. During the same period two small reservoirs were built at Roddlesworth to collect the water from the northern end of the moor and this water was brought round from them to the Anglezarke Reservoir by means of a channel known as the Goit. Even these vast supplies were not enough for Liverpool's growing population and a third reservoir was added at Roddlesworth in 1865 and the Yarrow Reservoir was built between 1871 and 1875. Today, these and all other reservoirs for drinking water are administered by the North West Water Authority. There are many small reservoirs serving former bleach and dye works that are privately owned. Fishing rights are leased to various angling clubs.

The three main reservoirs shelter a big population of wildfowl in winter, especially in the secluded and shallow north-eastern part of the Upper Rivington Reservoir. Mallard, tufted pochard, golden eye teal and other duck also great crested grebe can often be seen and sometimes whooper swans. At sunset on a winter's afternoon, they, together with seagulls, form large rafts in the centre of the Anglezarke Reservoir.

If you arrived by the road that passes the Yew Tree Inn, you could not fail to notice the old quarry workings. These are called Leicester Mill Quarries, but today the most prominent of them has been named Anglezarke Quarry by climbers, with whom it is very popular. It has one very famous climb called the Golden Tower. It is straight opposite and slightly to the right as you go in through either of the two gaps. It's very appropriately named, but you rarely see anyone climb it, it is so difficult. All these quarries produced stone setts for road making between 1880 and 1920. There are more climbs in the other quarry further along the bottom road that goes to High Bullough Reservoir. (Guidebook: *Rock Climbs in Lancashire and the North West* - published by Cicerone Press.)

If you want to look at Rivington village and the Hall Barn on this walk, see the notes to Walk No.1.4.

The green track that you follow up the fields from the bridge over the Yarrow Reservoir is part of the original road to Rivington. The present road was not built until after the reservoirs were built.

Manor House is a fine example of an early seventeenth century farmhouse. It was re-built by a Robert Shaw in 1604 and shows all the characteristics of a house of that period: large mullion windows with drip courses, big corner stones, and stones of decreasing sizes used on the upper courses. Originally it would have had a flag roof but it was re-roofed in the 1890's at the same time as the additions at the back were made.

The word 'Street' is often associated with the site of a Roman road, but there is no other evidence that one did in fact run along here, though there was a small farm hereabouts long before the building of the Victorian mansion now known as The Street and recently converted into flats. It was built in the 1850's by one Peter Martin, a Bolton man who was a J.P. for the County of Lancaster. He owned a large cotton spinning mill in Bolton employing over 400 people and farmed some 300 acres around his residence. 14 men and a boy were employed in the gardens around The Street. By 1881 the Martin family were no longer in residence there.

Looking over Anglezarke Reservoir to
Upper and Lower Rivington Reservoirs

The Waterman's Cottage

A WALK ROUND ANGLEZARKE RESERVOIR
WALK NO.**1.9**

This walk starts from the new car park at Leicester Mill Quarry and walks the banks as closely as possible. The views are best when done this way round.

You can if you like extend it to go round the Upper Rivington Reservoir or you can simply go there for bird watching.

Time: about 2 hours.

To find the new car park, turn up Babylon Lane at the lights on the A6, Adlington. Turn right at the first junction and left immediately you've crossed the M61. Take the right fork at the Yew Tree, and very shortly afterwards you will be on the reservoir embankment. Cross it, turn left at the road junction and continue to the new parking ground, which is straight ahead at the hairpin bend.

Leave the car park by a swing gate on the right at the top of the approach road and follow the new track waymarked with red topped posts down to the tarmac road. Stay on the tarmac until you have passed the big bay of the reservoir then cut across left as soon as convenient to the rough path that runs round the wooded headland. Follow it along the shore line until you re-join the main well main-

79

tained path. Turn left on this and follow it through a number of stiles to the road close to Waterman's Cottage. If you now find yourself short of time it is quicker to return by road from this point. Otherwise continue round the end of the reservoir on the road to its far corner by the wood. Cross the wooden stile and immediately turn left and follow the track along the wall. This is a good place to watch for duck and other water birds. At a fork take the right-hand one which brings you to a ladder stile, and having crossed the field you will enter a rough cart track which has very good views. Turn left and follow it to the road. Turn left on the road and follow it to the end of the reservoir embankment. Almost opposite a house there is a corner with a gate and stile. Go through this and follow this track first between walls and later divided into a whole lot of animal tracks. Keep to the reservoir side and then follow the wall and it will lead you to a stile onto the road. Then a good 10 minutes along it will see you back to your car. Alternatively if you go straight ahead into the private road leading to The Street you join Walk No.1.8.

(Things of interest - see the notes to the next walk.)

A WALK UP LEAD MINE VALLEY TO ROUND LOAF AND PIKESTONES   WALK NO.1.10

Lead Mine Valley takes it local name from the early lead mine workings there but on the O.S. map it is called Limestone Clough. It is one of the pleasantest wooded valleys on the western edge of the West Pennine Moors. The British Trust for Conservation Volunteers under the direction of the West Pennine Moors Management Committee have partially excavated and restored some of the mining features and provided an informative leaflet describing the Lead Mine Trail. It is available at the Great House Barn Information Centre.

Time: about 2½ hours, but only an hour if you just wish to have a look at Lead Mine Valley.

Park in the new car park at Leicester Mill Quarry. To find this, see the previous walk.

To start the walk, leave it as you drove in, turn left along the road, left at the triangular junction and follow the road to the swing gate in the corner at the bridge over the Yarrow Reservoir. If you only want to visit Lead Mine Valley, returning as you came, it may be possible to park in one of several small lay-bys on this road.

From the swing gate follow the path up this delightful wooded valley until it forks. Take the left-hand one, cross the bridge and

The Waterfall, Lead Mines Valley

immediately turn right through a swing gate. Follow the path by the stream. Almost at once you pass the excavated slime pit on your left, now rather overgrown, and opposite it at stream level is the South Sough, dug to drain the workings sometime towards the end of the eighteenth century. Ahead you will see the fenced enclosure where the water-wheel pit and the shaft have been excavated. Climb up to them and continue to the War Memorial above.

From here several tracks lead in different directions. Take the one that goes up the valley towards the new fence and follow it just below the fence until you can see the main cart track now re-surfaced with unpleasantly large stones as it is an access road in the new afforestation scheme. Join it and follow it up the valley and then onto the moor. This will take about 10 minutes. After a few minutes you will see Round Loaf ahead, but don't be tempted to make a bee-line for it. However wet the track, the moor is worse. Stay on the track until you've crossed the second grough. It can be difficult to cross and is easier upstream. Then make directly for Round Loaf.

The view of Winter Hill with its T.V. masts and Rivington Pike is very good. About half way between the two, on the highest point of the moor, you can just make out as a little pip the tumulus or burial cairn on Noon Hill. Whilst still looking this way, Devil's Dike is the second dark trench across the moor. A wet track goes most of the way to it, and if you decide to go that way, it's best to return direct to the main track from it.

To visit Pike Stones from here involves a bit of really rough moorland walking. First of all aim at the top of Hurst Hill. There's no path. Choose the side of any convenient drainage ditch, it's usually better going. You won't be able to see Pike Stones from the top of it, but face so that you are walking towards the embankment that separates the Anglezarke and Upper Rivington reservoirs. If you have a compass take a bearing of 200° from magnetic north. Then 10 minutes walk will see you at Pike Stones.

It used to be possible to follow a little track to a wall corner below you but now that simple route has been cut off by a substantial sheep netting fence topped with barbed wire that surrounds a large area of the moor being afforested. Continue facing the reservoirs and follow the line of the fence bearing right along tractor markings to a gate onto the rough stony track that runs into Lead Mine Valley. Turn right on it and follow it to the tarmac. Turn left here and follow it down the hill until you reach the top-side of the car park.

Then re-trace your steps, or take a short cut into it.

Things of Interest

Lead mining in Anglezarke has had a very chequered history. It started in 1693 when Peter Shaw, one of the local gentry, sought to retrieve the family's fortunes which had been lost after the Restoration of the Monarchy in 1660. The Shaws had been staunch Parliamentarians. He signed an agreement with Sir Richard Standish who owned the Manor of Anglezarke, to prospect for lead. Eventually they located a vein, not, it is thought in Lead Mine Valley itself, but over the shoulder of the hill overlooking the River Yarrow where two large spoil heaps remain to this day. The remains in Lead Mine Valley probably date from 1780 when Sir Frank Standish re-opened the mines, (they had been closed only a year or two after they were opened as Sir Richard had died). He sank new shafts and dug the South Sough drainage level.

At this time, the hey day of the mines, some 73 tons of lead were produced in 1788/9 and 10-16 miners were employed. Another important mineral, witherite, was also produced. In fact, Anglezarke

The Old Wheel Pit, Lead Mines Valley

83

was better known for its witherite than for its lead. Witherite is barium carbonate, quite a rare mineral, whilst lead was produced in great abundance in the Yorkshire Dales. Witherite takes its name from a Birmingham chemist, a Dr. Withering, who identified the mineral. It was used as a medicine, despite being extremely poisonous, and as an ingredient in porcelain manufacture. Josia Wedgewood records that he obtained his supplies from Andlesargh (the old spelling) near Chorley.

In the days before steam, machinery was generally worked by a water-wheel. The excavated wheel pit would have held a wheel some 20ft. in diameter and it took its water not from the stream but from a spring a little way up the hillside. The water was brought to the wheel in a wooden trough called a launder which was supported on stone pillars and then drained away into the stream from the bottom of the wheel pit. These pillars have been re-built. The wheel is thought to have been used to pump water from the shaft next to it as the workings were particularly troubled with water.

As the material that was mined only contained between 1 and 2% of lead ore, it was crushed and the galena or lead separated from it lower down the valley. The slime pit was part of the purification plant. Lead was not smelted on the site but the ore was sold to the London Lead Company who owned many of the lead smelting mills in the Yorkshire Dales. The mines were closed soon after this burst of activity and fell into ruin. A John Thompson of Wigan had a lease of them in 1829 and though he sank new shafts, failed to find more ore and withdrew in 1837. The mines were never worked again and the shafts were filled in sometime during the 1930s as part of a programme to find work for the many unemployed.

(If you want to know more about the techniques of lead mining and smelting in the Yorkshire Dales, which also apply to Anglezarke, see the author's book, *The Yorkshire Dales National Park: a guide for walkers.*)

As you pass below the fence just after leaving the War Memorial you are above a fine little waterfall. It is part of the Brinscall fault that caused the big escarpment of the western edge of the moors.

Round Loaf has never been excavated scientifically and its origin is somewhat uncertain. It is much too big for a Bronze Age burial mound and Neolithic mounds are usually long in shape (long barrows). Present thinking is that it is a round Neolithic barow of the type occasionally found in Wales, but until it is excavated the mystery cannot be resolved. With the present urgent need to investigate so many sites at risk in towns this is highly unlikely. In those times the whole area was lightly wooded and much more favourable for habitation by Man.

Devil's Dike is a long shallow trench in the moor easily visible from Round Loaf and marked on the map. It is sometimes considered to be an associated earthwork but the author believes that it is the remains of the boundary of a deer park which was in Anglezarke in the fourteenth century.

Pikestones is a chambered tomb of the gallery type dated roughly 3000-2000 B.C. and has a commanding view to the south. The elongated cairn is aligned NNW-SSE and was entered from the north. Only five stones of the chamber remain and originally it would have been covered with earth and turf which has weathered away. It was excavated and robbed of its grave goods at some time long past. Mounds like this were often family tombs with multiple burials.

A children's novel, *Grimsdyke*, by Walt Unsworth has many scenes set in the Rivington area including Lead Mine Valley, Winter Hill and Great Barn. Published by Gollancz it is out of print but can probably be obtained from libraries. It will add interest for any children walking in the area.

A WALK ROUND THE ANGLEZARKE WOODLAND TRAIL
WALK NO.1.11

This walk goes through the old quarries then round the High Bullough Reservoir and returns along the banks of the Anglezarke Reservoir. It is waymarked with red ringed stakes but unlike some nature trails does not have a series of stations where something of special interest may be seen. In fact, there is something of interest all the time, and even if you are not interested in the natural history aspect, it is a very pleasant walk indeed, taking about 1 hour. Suitable for shoes in dry weather.

Start at the car park at Leicester Mill Quarry. See Walk No.1.9 for instructions for finding it and leave the car park as for that walk. After you've gone along the tarmac for a little way look for a marker that directs you into the old quarry on the right.

Here heather and bilberry grow profusely and blackberries may be found in season. Small willow, birch and oak trees are spread around, self sown seedlings from the nearby woodlands. The quarry face shows something of the geology of the area - horizontal beds of a rather smooth gritstone covered with a thick layer of shale. This quarry was developed at the time the reservoirs were built (1850-55) when vast amounts of stone were needed for pitching of the banks, wall building and other associated works. Later the stone was used for setts and curbstones for roads and the quarry ceased to be worked in the 1920 s. It takes its name from Lester Mill, (Leicester is a modern variation) now lost under the waters of the reservoir. Lester Mill was the Manor Corn Mill in the 16th, 17th and 18th centuries and in the 16th century one Robert Lester was the miller. It is said that it became a textile mill and although it was common for a corn mill to be converted to a water-powered textile mill, there is no evidence that this was done here.

Continue through the quarry to regain the road and carry on until another red topped stake guides you onto a footpath on the right which will take you up to the High Bullough Reservoir. The path goes behind the reservoir giving you a good position for bird watching and at the end crosses the stream by a footbridge. Now turn left and follow the path down to a much wider path.

The High Bullough wood which you pass through is a piece of old woodland containing many mature sycamore, beech and oak trees. Of these only the oak is a local native tree. The beech is native to the limestone ares of southern England and the sycamore was introduced in Tudor times. Woodland plants nearly always flower in the spring-time before the trees are in full leaf as they need the light which is cut off by the leaves. They are often moisture loving plants as well and you may find, amongst others, red campion, stitchwort, golden saxifrage, bluebells, foxgloves, woodsage and forget-me-not. Woodland provides a good habitat for birds and besides the common ones of the urban gardens, the chaffinches, thrushes, blackbirds, robins and tits, you may see the sleek willow warblers, tree creepers, red starts, jays and woodpeckers. On the reservoir itself you may see golden eye duck, little grebes and other waterfowl in winter, and in summer the common sandpiper can be seen - and heard, for they have a loud piping cry, hence the name.

The High Bullough reservoir takes its name from the original name, the true name, of Manor House Farm which stands on the road above it. Bullough is an old Anglezarke family name and until about 1890 Manor House was called High Bullough Farm. This reservoir was built in 1846-48 by a private company, Chorley Waterworks, to supply Chorley. It took water from Lead Mine Valley well above the old workings and brought it by an open channel that contoured Twitch-ell's Brook to the road close to the Viewpoint car park and from there straight down by a pipeline to the reservoir below. From the reservoir water was taken by pipeline over Healey Nab (the reservoir is higher than the Nab) and then into Chorley where it was distributed to what may best be called stand-pipes.

Here turn right and turn left at the waymarker about 50yds. further on and follow the path right round the shore of the reservoir until you rejoin the tarmac road. Turn right and continue along the road. A waymarker and sign show you where to leave it and climb up to the car park.

As you join the wide path you pass the remains of Brook House Farm. It is known that this farm was in existence at the beginning of the seventeenth century, and probably four hundred years before that. The plantation takes its name from the farm. The trees, mostly beech, were planted soon after the Anglezarke Reservoir was built in order to stabilize the ground. Today they are mature and because of grazing sheep have not been able to regenerate themselves. Recently the land has been fenced to keep sheep out and young native trees - oak, rowan, alder, holly, birch - have been planted so that in time they may replace this piece of woodland which is slowly dying.

GREAT HILL AND THE ANGLEZARKE MOORS
WALK NO.1.12

Great Hill isn't even given a spot height on the map. It's about 365 metres or 1,200ft. high, a good viewpoint, and a very easy climb from White Coppice. It can also be taken in your stride on the two longer walks described here.

Time just to do Great Hill: 1¼-1½ hours return.

To find White Coppice turn off the Chorley-Blackburn road (A675) at Lower Wheelton - it's signposted Heapey, turn left by the Railway Inn, bear left over the little bridge by the cottages, and turn left into the cinder track. This leads to the cricket pitch - surely there is no prettier cricket pitch in the whole of Lancashire - and this together with the setting of the row of old, picturesque cottages by the reservoir make a visit to White Coppice worthwhile even if you don't want to climb Great Hill. Park by the cricket pitch or on the wide part of the cinder track.

Cross the Goit by the stone bridge, turn sharp left as soon as you're through the swinging gate, and sharp right at the Ramblers Association signpost. A broad, well-marked track leads you unmistakably to the top. If it's clear the view is similar to that from the Pike, but it's not so easy to see North Wales. On the other hand you can see the Lakes more easily to the left of the Bowlands, and Pendle Hill separat-

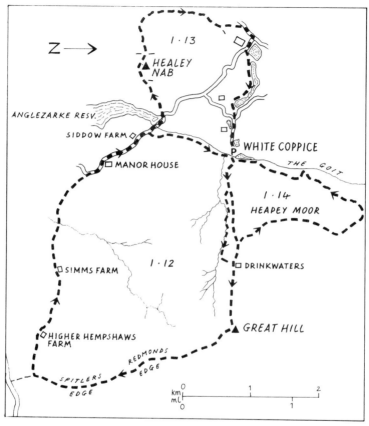

ing the Ribble and Calder valleys. Darwen Tower cuts off any view further right than this, though you can just see the top part of Bull Hill, the highest part in the eastern section of the West Pennine Moors Area, in the dip between Darwen Moor and Turton Moor. It's not very often the industrial valleys are sufficiently clear of haze and smoke to give these views to the east.

From the top there's a choice of ways back besides just retracing your steps all the way. The most pleasant one is to retrace your steps just to Drinkwaters Farm, the last derelict farm on the way up. At the beginning of the trees you will find a little track going off to the left and leading down to the edge of the stream. There you will find another little track leading right down the stream. It enters a fine little gorge, crosses the stream once or twice, and finally comes out on the steep bit of the hill above White Coppice.

A more ambitious circuit goes over Redmonds and Spitlers Edges almost to the Belmont-Rivington road, turns down the infant River Yarrow by a pair of derelict farms, from there crosses over to Lead Mine Valley, and climbs up to Jepsons Gate on the road that runs round Anglezarke, and returns to White Coppice by the Goit woods. Time to return to White Coppice: about 2½ hours.

The details of this are as follows: From the top of Great Hill continue in the direction of Darwen Tower for about 100 yards. Here, on the right, there is a branch track. Take this, cross the fence at the stile and follow the well defined track that runs along the top of the moor to the Rivington-Belmont road. There's two awkward places if it's wet, deep cut groughs or trenches in the peat. It's easier to cross further left, but take care to return to the main track. On a good day this gives first-rate moorland walking. When you are coming down the last bit of steepish hill to the road, and you're within a few hundred yards of it, look for a faint track going off to the right. It runs along a ridge 4-5ft.

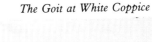

The Goit at White Coppice

wide and about a foot high. A different sort of grass grows on it, much shorter and greener than the surroundings. It is important to start correctly or you will find some very hard going over big tussocks.

The ridge soon disappears, but the track runs quite distinctly down to Higher Hempshaw's. Cross the stream just below it, where you will find a newly made cart track which goes round to Simms. It gives tedious and uncomfortable walking on its large stones, so follow it as far as the ruins of Lower Hempshaw's, just ahead. As soon as you have gone through the gateway at the end of the ruined buildings, turn right and immediately go through another gateway in the wall. Follow this wall, ignoring a wide groove in the grass to the right which looks like a cart track. The track you want has disappeared temporarily and it appears better to go straight on, but don't be tempted. In about 200 yards there is another wall and from the gap in it you will see the track quite clearly winding its way across the moor to Simms. In late summer it will be overgrown with tall grass and not be so easy to follow. At Simms you join the cart track mentioned earlier and follow this down to Lead Mine Valley. Cross the stream by the bridge to the right and follow the cart track right to the road above Manor House. Turn right and follow the road past Manor House and Siddow Farm to the bottom of the hill near the reservoir. On the right go through the swing gate and bear left to the corner of the wood, then make for the stony cart track ahead. Follow this to White Coppice. You can take a useful short cut by following a narrow but well trodden path on the left a few yards after the cart track swings to the right.

Things of Interest Seen on these Moors

There seems to be more derelict farms in this part of the moors than almost anywhere else. Now very little remains of any of them and it is hard to see how anybody could have made a living there. Drinkwaters, with its belt of sheltering sycamore trees is the most prominent. Approaching it, as soon as you are through the gateway by the R.A. signpost, you can see a row of mine spoil heaps on the right running down to the stream. These are the remains of some old shafts dug in the early part of the nineteenth century to exploit a vein of galena, one of the ores of lead. A little further on you pass the spring from which the farm took its water supply, just below on the right. There's a trough in a recess built of stones in the crevices of which the little Hard fern grows. Ferns are rare on moorlands because they need shade and drainage which here are provided by the recess. Round Loaf can be seen across the stream on the right from this point. You can visit it on the return trip using the track from Drinkwaters to the stream, but there is no track up the other side for quite a way and it's hard going. (See Walk No.1.10 for more information.)

Once you've gone through the top gate you'll see it's mostly bare peat underfoot. This peat layer blankets a large part of these moors. It only forms in regions of high rainfall - more than 60 inches (150cms.) - per annum, and low temperatures. It is formed from decaying vegetation and increases at the rate of 2 inches (5cms.) per 100 years. Deep layers have been found to contain pollen grains of birch and alder, sure evidence of a warmer climate in times past. Today trees will only grow on the lower slopes or where there is some shelter; for example, the beech trees by the stream below Drinkwaters. This copse contains quite a variety of trees. There are a few small sycamores, a couple of Scots pines, and a little further down, a willow and a splendid specimen of a rowan or mountain ash. Only the sycamore seems to be sufficiently hardy to grow in the windiest places. Black Dean brook cuts quite a little gorge for itself through the soft beds of shale, geologically the same as those in Lead Mine Valley. The War Memorial in Lead Mine Valley was erected by Horwich Rotary Club in memory of the crew of a Wellington bomber that crashed on these moors in 1943.

The Goit is an artificial stream built to bring water from the Roddlesworth Reservoir at Tockholes to the Anglezarke Reservoir. In its clear waters fingerling trout may sometimes be seen. Dragon flies can occasionally be seen whilst ring ouzel, dipper, and stonechat frequent its banks which are thick with blackberry, meadow sweet and other moisture loving plants. In one place there is a stand of Himalayan Balsam, a very tall plant with thick stems, big leaves and an exotic looking pinkish flower. It seems to be spreading quite fast, though it was once quite rare.

A number of the farms at White Coppice are listed buildings, as are also Manor House Farm and Siddows Farm.

HEALEY NAB FROM WHITE COPPICE   WALK NO.1.13

Healey Nab is the low hill slightly left of centre when looking towards the coast from White Coppice. The walk has considerable variety and good views from the Nab on a clear day.

Time: 2 hours or a little more.

Park at the cricket pitch, White Coppice. To find this, see the previous walk.

Start as for the previous walk but turn right as soon as you have crossed the Goit. Follow the stony cart track that winds along the flat valley bottom until it comes to the road just beyond the Waterman's Cottage on the banks of the Anglezarke Reservoir. (There are two corner cutting short cuts on grassy tracks that are well worthwhile in dry conditions. The first is on the right as soon as you have crossed the railway sleeper bridge a few hundred yards after starting, the second follows the wall which you reach in 10 or 15 minutes.) Turn right on the road and follow it for about a quarter of a mile to a sharp right-hand bend. Here go straight ahead up a set of steps through the beech wood to a stile that brings you into a couple of rough fields. Keep straight ahead to the top of the Nab marked by a substantial cairn.

The Lancashire plain is now spread before you. Chorley is just beyond Talbot Mill, once a large spinning and weaving complex built in 1910 and still working. Far beyond you may locate the gasometer (ugh!) at Southport or even, well to the right, Blackpool Tower on a really clear day. Behind you there are good views of the Pike and Winter Hill and its collection of masts.

From the cairn go steeply down the wall side and over its end onto a wide grassy cart track. Opposite a stile takes you down to the Nab Spout, one of the many springs found at the foot of steep slopes in the Pennines. Usually it is too boggy to cross below the spring, so climb up the bank to go over it. Then go down the hillside on a well trodden track to its junction with a cinder track only a field's length away from Talbot Mill. Turn right and right again in a few yards onto another cinder track. Follow this to an isolated cottage where it becomes a field path that leads to a short row of houses and then the road.

Turn right on the road and right again at the junction just beyond the industrial area, the site of Heapey Bleach Works. About 100yds. up this road just beyond a small car park on the left, a footpath goes up the banking through a band of shrubs onto the bank of a small reservoir. Now go over the stile on the right and along the length of the reservoir bank. On a clear day there are fine views of the moors behind White Coppice. At the end of this reservoir go straight ahead over a decrepit stile onto the banks of yet another reservoir and follow them, then the inlet stream by a well marked path to the road opposite the former Sunday School at White Coppice. Turn right on the road, bear left over the bridge and continue onto the cinder track and the cricket pitch.

Things of Interest

The Waterman's Cottage is a mock Tudor house built by Liverpool

Corporation about 1855 to house the waterman who inspected the installations.

The banks of the reservoirs you walk along on your return to White Coppice once formed part of the water supply for Heapey Bleach Works, long since defunct. Now they are a good place for flowers. In August you will find marsh woundwort, common skull cap, great willow herb as well as the more common rosebay willow herb, water mint, and in the water itself, the common burr reed. Hemlock water dropwort, a most poisonous plant, grows on the bank of the upper reservoir close to where the stream flows in. Along the stream you will find in June pink bistort, the occasional flag iris, and brooklime, a bright blue flower rather like a forget-me-not but having only four petals not five. Near the bridge there is a white flower, rather like candytuft. This is hairy bittercress, a relation of watercress but not edible. As you go past the row of old cottages close to the stream be sure to look over the wall to see the well-kept garden of the end one, a real treat for garden lovers. 140 or so years ago one of these cottages was a blacksmith's shop. Soon after you have passed the White Coppice Meeting Room and just below the next reservoir, you pass the site of the White Coppice Cotton Mill. It was demolished in the early 1920's and scarcely anything remains now. See the *Industrial History of White Coppice* for more about this aspect of the hamlet.

HEAPEY MOOR AND BRINSCALL WOODS   WALK NO.1.14

Park at the cricket pitch, White Coppice. See Walk No.1.12 for instructions for finding it.

   Time: about 2 hours. Add on ¾ hour if you put in Great Hill as an optional extra.

   Start as for Walk No.1.12 but when you have reached the top of the steep rise onto the moor and found the end of the quarry fence bear right on to a narrow but well trodden path that takes a level course to the stream. Now follow the stream, crossing and re-crossing several times, not always easily, until you reach a well-fenced old mine shaft just above the stream. Now leave the stream and go uphill towards a clump of beech trees, there's no path and it is rather rough going, but it doesn't last long. You will soon reach the main path to Great Hill used on Walk No.1.12. Turn right if you want to put in the optional extra. Otherwise turn left and bear right at the Ramblers' Association finger post about 100yds. further on. This cart track has some very wet places on it at the beginning, but they can all be avoided with care.

Follow it over the moor to a wall corner then bear right and follow the wall until the cart track meets the rough road that climbs up the moor from Brinscall. Turn left here and go down the road to a swing gate by a clump of tall pine trees on your left. This gate is not very obvious but puts you onto a wide cart track that leads through the woods though it becomes a mere footpath towards the end. Follow it all the way to a lane that crosses the Goit. Opposite you will see a stile. Cross this and make diagonally left to a row of holly trees. Here a path is well defined if muddy and you can follow it easily back to its junction with the Great Hill path and in sight of your car.

Things of Interest

Possibly one of the most interesting walks in the whole book. Black Dean Brook forms a gorge which is only passable by the young and athletic but the path described leads in above these difficulties. The gorge was formed by faulting brought about by earth movements some 250 million years ago. Faulting leaves a band of broken rock that is easily scoured away by water and so leaves a steep sided trench which can be seen downstream from the point where you join it. A little higher up the stream has cut through the rock strata of the Coal Measures leaving a 30ft. high bank of shale and rock topped by a few feet of glacial deposits and a few inches of peat.

The fenced mine shaft is one of a series that run up the hill following a vein of lead bearing rock. Their surrounding spoil heaps make them easy to see. Bear in mind that they too have a shaft in the bottom of the depression, and like the one by the river, it might collapse under your weight. That shaft just appeared as a hole in the ground one day! Brinscall woods are particularly interesting, not just for their birds and their bluebells. Before the reservoirs and the Goit were built in 1857 this was farm land. The remains of many small buildings can be seen just as you enter the wood. Trees were planted to stabilize the ground and minimize the risk of landslides. As you reach the highest point on the track you will see the remains of a large house on your left. This was Heatherlea, built about 1875 and lived in until the 1930's. Old photographs show it with double fronted bay windows. A little further on are the scant remains of another house with its terraced gardens, and below the path not at all easy to find, an underground cowshed of unusual design still with its stalls made of flags. It seems likely that it had a hay barn above and was associated with this house.

WALKS ROUND JUMBLES, WAYOH AND ENTWISTLE RESERVOIR

JUMBLES COUNTRY PARK

Jumbles Country Park is the only Country Park within the West Pennine Moors Recreation Area at present, though others are planned, and it owes its existence to the far sightedness of Turton R.D.C. It is quite a small Country Park embracing only the reservoir and its immediate surroundings. The footpath around it has been re-made and gives easy dry walking suitable for shoes at all times of the year. It has been set out as a nature trail and is described in a leaflet covering Jumbles Country Park, price 15p. It also has a considerable geological interest. Coarse fishing is allowed there and licences are available from the NWWA. Wayoh and Entwistle reservoirs are managed as trout fisheries, again by licence. Jumbles Sailing Club uses the southern part of the reservoir and has a club house best reached from Horrobin Lane.

Approaches to Jumbles

The Waterfold car park on the bank of the reservoir is easily reached from the Bolton-Burnley road, the A676. If you are coming from Bolton turn left down a lane immediately after two detached brick houses on the right. If you are coming from the Blackburn direction, take the first right after the Lamb Inn, about a mile. The signs at the lane end are small and difficult to see. The car park has toilets, map board, shop and Information Centre, open only on Wednesday afternoons and, at weekends at present.

There is also a car park at Ousel Nest about a mile beyond Bromley Cross Station on the B6391. It is well signed. To reach Jumbles Reservoir from it, follow the wide fenced path down to Grange Road (the narrow one leads to a play area). Go straight across this rough road and follow the obvious path quite steeply down to the bridge over Bradshaw Brook. Then follow the steps up to the Waterfold car park. It will take about 20 minutes.

If you come by public transport, Bromley Cross Station on the Blackburn/Bolton line is only 15 minutes walk away. Leave the station on the opposite side from the car parking area, turn right and immediately left into Grange Road. Continue left along it for about 5 minutes then keep a look out for a pair of fluted iron gate posts in the hedge on the right. They mark the start of the path that leads quite plainly to the Waterfold car park. If you want to visit Wayoh or Entwistle reservoir Entwistle Station is equally useful.

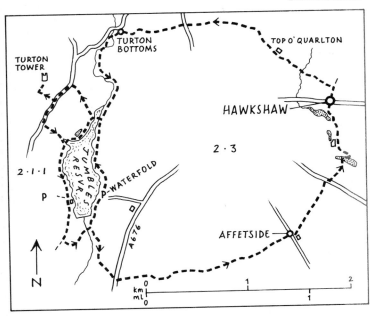

Using the bus, the Bolton-Burnley service No.273 passes the lane leading to Waterfold car park (5 min. walk), and the Bolton-Edgworth No.563 and Bolton-Bury via Edgworth No.565 pass the Ousel Nest car park.

ROUND THE RESERVOIR   WALK NO.2.1.1

Allow about an hour. A wide gravel path runs most of the way round the reservoir and gives pleasant easy walking. Points to watch: cross the bridge (extension to Turton Tower starts here - see below) and then turn left onto the other bank. After passing a row of cottages you will join a cobbled lane. Leave it on the left crossing an arm of the reservoir, then go through a field into a stable yard and on into a tree-lined avenue. At its end there is a brick built house with a black and white upper storey. The path to Ousel Nest car park is on the right in about 100yds., opposite the next house, but if you started from Waterfold continue for another 200yds. or so to a signed path that will take you back there.

Extension to Turton Tower

Allow an extra 30 minutes plus such time as you spend at the Tower. See page 29 for notes on the Tower.

Keep straight ahead when you have crossed the bridge. The path goes through the wood into pastures, wet in bad weather, and goes directly to the road. Turn left and the entrance is about 200yds. along the road. It is well signed. When you leave the Tower turn right on the road and after a good hundred yards turn left into Horrobin Lane. Follow this cobbled lane to the path around the reservoir and continue along it to the right to complete the circuit.

Jumbles Geology

The pamphlet describing the nature trail gives a brief account of the geology of the area and one or two things may be added to it. The path leading from Waterfold car park is surfaced with crushed gritstone and is a modern addition, but near the first bay where Horrobin Mill is submerged, the surface of the original lane leading to it is still visible. It was made of boulder clay, excavated probably when the small reservoir above the mill was made. This clay contains large numbers of glacial erratics, big pebbles of granite and slate from the Lake District, quite distinctive. The quarry face seen from the bridge shows two very distinct rock types, but there are more. The upper strata has bands of a brown mudstone and black shale, the latter so thinly bedded they are known as paper shales. Some of these bands contain marine fossils and there is an extremely thin band of coal. These 'rocks' - if that is the word to describe a material so crumbly that it can easily be broken in the fingers of one hand - have weathered and caused the scree slopes immediately below them. Below these is a band of massive coarse sandstone, called Rough Rock and below that, only visible if the water level is down, is a band of coal, formerly mined hereabouts. All these rocks were laid down some 300 million years ago as the delta of a huge fast flowing river, the Great Upper Carboniferous Delta. The coarse grained rock was laid down when the river was in flood, probably when it broke its banks. The fine particles of the mudstones were deposited slowly from still water, probably in a lagoon left when the river changed its course after the floods. These paper shales were deposited very slowly whilst the coarse rocks very quickly indeed. There is unusual evidence of speedy deposition in the form of a fossil tree, still upright, embedded in the upper rock. As trees quickly fall over when they die this suggests that this tree was engulfed whilst it was still alive. All of these deposits have been compressed by their own weight over the millions of years that have passed since that time to form the rocks today.

If you parked at Ousel Nest there is more of geological interest in the quarry below. The car park did not take its name from some long lost blackbird but from this quarry, Ousel Nest Quarry, whose name is preserved for evermore in the annals of geology by the use of its name to characterize one of the many types of gritstone to be found in the locality, Ousel Nest Grit. The quarry came to the end of its useful life many years ago. Its floor has been levelled and grassed over as a play area, but at the far left-hand end, if approached down the steps, below a shale band, there is an example of cross bedding caused by a change in the direction of flow of the river delta. Beyond, almost the entire quarry face shows many areas of smooth almost horizontal scratches. These have been caused by what is called slickenside faulting, a side-ways movement of the rock strata instead of the more usual vertical movement. The scratches are smooth because the rock was partially melted by the friction heat that developed. This huge quarry was worked before the days of drag lines and JCB's mainly by men using hand tools and they were able to do so because they exploited the weakness of slickenside faulting. Today it is used by rock climbers for practice.

Wayoh Reservoir

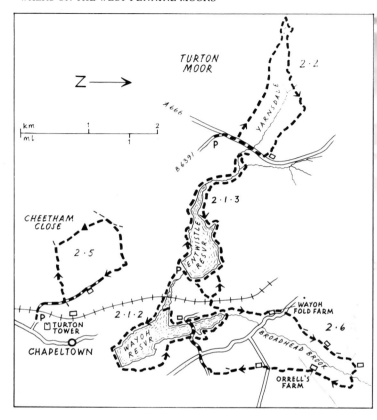

AROUND WAYOH RESERVOIR   WALK NO.2.1.2

A large new car park has been built just below the dam of the Entwistle Reservoir and it is linked to Wayoh Reservoir by a new concessionary path of great beauty. To find this car park, take the minor road, the B6391 from Bradshaw, Bolton, through Bromley Cross and Chapeltown. When you have crossed the railway cutting take the first road on the right, in about a quarter of a mile. It is signed as 'no through road' and takes you to the dam and car park, which is out of sight on the right as you approach. The walk is suitable for

100

shoes and any weather, and can be done either way round equally well.

Time: about 1½ hours-2 hours depending on the return.

From the right-hand corner of the new car park follow the new path, neatly gravelled and provided with steps and bridges, down the wooded valley passing under the railway viaduct to the path that crosses the causeway. Turn right here and follow the well made path along the shores of the reservoir to the dam. Cross the dam, and although a track continues along the bank to the upper dam, in 1986 it was diverted into the fields above. Turn right and find this diversion a mere 50 yards away. Follow it by the fence back to the water side again. When you reach the upper dam you have a choice of ways.

a)the shortest return, about 25 minutes back to your car. Cross the dam and at the bend of the road ahead turn left as if you were going to the farm, then immediately turn left again onto a footpath that follows the water's edge to the causeway. Cross it and you rejoin your outward route.

b)a continuation round the upper part, possibly the best part of the walk, and again, this offers a choice of return paths. The short one takes 45 minutes. Go straight across the road at the dam and when you have crossed two wooden bridges turn left and stay on the wide main track. It brings you onto the road at the end of the dam and you finish by (a) above.

The longer one will take just about an hour. After the second bridge leave the track that encircles the reservoir and climb up a wide grassy cart track bearing left through the wood into the fields and a stile just below the Strawberry Duck. Turn right and when you reach the pub keep straight on into Entwistle Lane. About 400 yards past the last house turn left up some steps leading to a fenced path that cuts through the trees to the bank of Entwistle Reservoir. Turn left on the rough road and follow it back to the car park.

ROUND ENTWISTLE RESERVOIR   WALK NO.2.1.3

Park at the car park used for the previous walk.

Time: about 1 hour. Suitable for shoes and any weather.

Start at the gate in the embankment wall near where you are parked. This path along the south side quickly establishes the character of the reservoir as a moorland one, quite different from the Wayoh. Turton Moor at the head is framed by steep tree-lined valley sides. The path all the way is straightforward and unmistakable. It crosses the inflow stream by a bridge. (This walk may be extended from this point. Add

45 minutes to the time.) Having crossed the bridge turn right and follow the path which becomes a cart track right up the valley. There are good views of Cadshaw Rocks, popular on summer evenings with local climbers. The cart track continues past the long disused Cadshaw quarry and winds its way round the shoulder of the hill and eventually reaches the A666 road. About 400 yards before reaching it - cars can easily be seen - a wide well marked path comes in on the left by a defunct notice board. Turn onto it and follow it back down the hill enjoying good views of Holcombe Moor and Tower. After going down a long flight of steps you join your outward path just above the bridge and return by the water's edge on the other side of the stream. Later the path leaves the water's edge to join a cinder track. This brings you back to the dam on the other side of which you are parked.

LINKING THESE WALKS
Wayoh and Entwistle
You will perceive that it is easy to link the walks round Wayoh and Entwistle reservoirs. It is best done by turning right instead of left where you join the Entwistle Reservoir bank after passing the Strawberry Duck and doing the Entwistle Reservoir in reverse. A fine varied walk of about 3 hours.

Jumbles and Wayoh
If you want to link these it is best to park at Waterfold car park. Start as for the first walk and continue as far as the footbridge. Here keep straight on following the stream up to Turton Bottoms, a picturesque collection of former mill cottages. Bear right into a former mill yard and then left across the bridge. When you are about 100 yards from the tarmac road turn right into a wide cinder track between two large houses, cross the bridge flanked by stout iron railings and continue to a cobbled lane, Birch Road. Turn right and at the end of the row of cottages keep straight on passing three decrepit buildings, the ruins of Black Rock Bleach Works. At the end of the last one turn right and then immediately left onto a wide track that climbs steeply up the bank. It passes below an isolated chimney, (marked on the map) a relic of the former industry below and keeps below the farm to drop down to a footbridge. Cross it and turn right and then follow this very pleasant path through the woods, colourful with rhododendrons in June.

Keep right at the fork. You will join an old walled lane just below the school, turn left into a field and follow the wall to the stile where a fenced (and nettley) strip of path takes you onto the road. Turn left and as soon as you have passed the garage, spare a moment for a look

The Railway Bridge, Wayho Reservoir

Holcombe Hill with Peel's Monument behind the
Turton and Entwistle Reservoir

at Brantwood Fold. There is a very fine Tudor house with mullioned
windows and perhaps more remarkable, a plaque on the gable end
stating that this house was the birthplace of Sir Thomas Barlow,
1845-1945, surgeon to Queen Victoria, King Edward VII and King
George V. Now cross the road and turn into Harbour Lane. At the
end of the short row of new houses there is a stile on the left. The next
stile gives a surprise view of the railway aqueduct across the Wayoh
Reservoir below and leads you at once to the path above the fence.
Turn right and join the circuit of the reservoir previously described
using the short finish as far as the causeway.

When you have reached the lower dam turn right onto the road.
Turn left and wander through Chapeltown, a Conservation Area with
some fine houses and associations with Sir Humphrey Chetham of
Chetham's Hospital fame. Keep straight on at the road junction for
about 400 yards when you will see a footpath sign on you left. Turn
left and follow the path over the hill and through the trees to the head
of Jumbles Reservoir and complete your circuit.

Things of Interest Seen on these Walks
The History of these Reservoirs
These three reservoirs whose banks offer so much attractive and easy
walking have been built over the last 150 years. The first one was the
Entwistle Reservoir, built in 1831 in order to ensure a steady water
supply for the bleach works further down Bradshaw Brook. It was
enlarged in 1840 and bought by compulsory purchase by Bolton

Corporation in 1863 to supply the town with water. Wayoh first came into use as a compensation reservoir to supply the bleach works that had the right to use water from Entwistle Reservoir. Wayoh's capacity was doubled in 1962 and the extra water used for public consumption. In 1971 when Jumbles was opened it took over the task of supplying compensation water thus allowing Wayoh to be fully utilized for drinking water. Today Entwistle and Wayoh supply over half of Bolton's drinking water. The rest comes from the Delph Reservoir and from Thirlmere. In past times Bradshaw Brook supplied the fulling mills and bleach works in the valley. Horrobin Mill, now beneath the waters of Jumbles Reservoir, was one of them. It was closed in 1941 and demolished in 1948. There is a collection of artefacts found during the making of the Jumbles Reservoir in the Information Centre.

Natural History

Jumbles Reservoir has its nature trail, somewhat heavily weighted towards trees, but the upper arm of Wayoh Reservoir gives a sheltered spot for many of the commoner flowers that can be found in the Area. Amongst them you may find: In spring; celandine, hundreds of them; marsh marigolds; butterburr; daisies; flowering currant, a garden escape; common scurvey grass - not a grass and not so common; bluebells; buttercups; ladies mantle; dandelion; horses tail -an unusual sort of plant, a bit like a branch off a pine tree with a sort of cone for a flower. In summer: meadow sweet; rosebay willow herb; bistort; blackberry; wild raspberry; common comfrey.

In contrast, the Turton and Entwistle reservoirs, being moorland in character and lined with Scots fir plantations, do not have a very varied collection of flowers. Heather and bilberries are common.

You may see duck, coots, jack snipe and other water birds on these reservoirs. In the woods around Turton and Entwistle reservoirs there are robins, wrens, cole, blue and great tits, linnets, jays and magpies. Dragon flies and damsel flies may be seen near the smaller reservoirs around Jumbles. Damsel flies look like tiny dragon flies. Some have bright blue bodies and are easily spotted as they look for all the world like flying blue matches. Others have red or brown bodies and are not so easily seen.

If you are interest in old buildings it is worth a small diversion to have a look at Entwistle Hall, which is in Entwistle Lane just below the Strawberry Duck. It is a fine stone built place, characteristic of the best of the old farm buildings in the 'Bolton Uplands'. It is a Grade 2 listed buildings.

Cadshaw Valley

A WALK ROUND CADSHAW (YARNSDALE)   WALK NO.2.2

This walk goes round the upper valley of the stream that flows into Entwistle Reservoir. It is a walk amongst the high pastures rather than on the moor and the effects of land reclamation from the moor can be seen quite strikingly at all times of the year. The walk can also be done as an extension to the extension of Walk No.2.1.3, and if you park at the new car park at Entwistle Reservoir you can have a whole after-noon's easy walking, returning by the bridleway used in the Three Towers walk. The walk as described will take only about 1½ hours.

To find a place to park if you are approaching from the Bolton side, look for the minor road that leaves it just on the north side of the Charters Moss Plantation, turn to the right down this and park in a lay-by. Return to the main road and continue about 100 yards further up the road to a gate and a stile. The cart track climbs gently up the side of the valley, passing a pond on the right where water crowfoot grows. There are one or two side tracks but ignore these until you come to one marked by the remains of a tall finger post now lying on the ground. Take the right-hand one: the left-hand one ends at some old coal pits whose spoil heaps are quite close. Your track quickly

106

becomes a thready little thing. Follow it carefully to the stream where there is a bridge. You need that bridge to cross the stream because right down this valley it is enclosed in vertical stone walls that make crossing very difficult indeed. Once you're across, climb steeply up to the cart track and turn right. If you turn left, you go either to Darwen or Belmont. Follow the cart track through a gate and up the hill. Turn right at the wall and continue to follow the track, now rather faint. It drops down the flank of the valley and continues as a well-marked cart track right to the road. As you pass the ruins of a farm look down to the right. Partly hidden by a clump of trees you will see the arch of the bridge on the old Bolton-Blackburn road. If you are parked in the minor road, turn right and 10 minutes will see you back to your car. If you have parked at Entwistle Reservoir turn left on the road and take the bridleway on the right in about 200 yards.

The cart tracks up the valley were once used to bring coal from the mines on the moors. At one time there were coke ovens at the collieries just above where you turn right. There are still fragments of coke and bricks lying round. The cart tracks are quite well supplied with springs and wells where today you will see water crowfoot growing. It flowers in early summer and must have shallow water to grow. It is no relation of the watercress and is not edible.

A WALK FROM JUMBLES RESERVOIR ROUND AFFETSIDE, HAWKSHAW AND TURTON BOTTOMS　　　WALK NO.2.3

A splendid walk in very varied surroundings and having good views.
　　Time for the circuit: 2½-3 hours. Light boots are recommended except in very dry weather as there are some wet and muddy fields.
　　Park at the Waterfold car park on Jumbles Reservoir. If you are coming from Bolton on the A676 turn left down a lane just after two detached brick houses on the right. If you are coming from Blackburn take the first turn on the right after the Lamb Inn. There are only very small signs for Jumbles Reservoir at the end of this lane.
　　Leave the car park by the far corner nearest the reservoir and follow the footpath until you are below the old quarry but well above the footbridge. Now turn left into a not very obvious lane, follow it to the road, cross the road and go up the lane opposite. This has been given new metal stiles and gates and leads to the Water Authority's treatment plant. The right of way has been diverted round the right-hand side, and isn't very clear. However, when you've passed the new metal fence slant leftwards to the wall where you will pick up the old

track again. It continues between two walls for a little way, then gets a bit difficult to follow when the walls end. Keep in the same general direction and you'll find it again by the next wall and that will lead you straight to Affetside. Turn left on the road if you want to look at the Headless Cross, one of the Ancient Monuments of the Area. It's about 50 yards down the road.

The Pack Horse Inn is almost straight opposite you when you come to the road, and the path you want goes down by the side of it. Turn right when you reach the road, cross it, and almost at once turn left down a footpath marked by a finger post. This takes you most pleasantly through hay fields, by the side of a small reservoir. When you have passed the reservoir the path is faint for a little while. Bear left, going quite steeply downhill and it soon becomes very good again, bringing you on to a cart track. Turn right here and then take the left fork and you will be in Hawkshaw in another 5 minutes.

Go straight across the road into Hawkshaw Lane. Follow it past the new houses, about 100 yards to a lane on the left with a footpath signpost. A little way along this, just before a wooden lock-up garage, turn left onto a not very obvious footpath that runs besides the houses into the field. Follow the hedge down to a bridge, cross it, then turn left and follow the hedge towards the house on the hillside above. There's no path but you will find a stile in the corner just below the house and almost at once another one taking you below the garden wall of the house. (This can be well-grown with nettles in summer, take a stick to beat them down.) When you reach the house, a well-built stone one with a date stone 1672 and a fine garden, go straight ahead up a sunken lane on its right. On the road at the top turn right and follow it into the yard of Top o' Quarlton, another fine old house. At the end of the yard go through a small gate into the field and follow the fence to the stile. The next three stiles are all in line from here but in summer these fields are hay meadows. Then walk round the left-hand boundaries rather than spoil the long grass by walking through it. The third stile puts you opposite a gate onto a good cart track one field's length from the road. At the road go straight across onto a signed field path. Follow it right down the hedge side to a stile at the top of a long flight of steps. They bring you into Turton Bottoms by the side of Quarlton Vale Bleach Works, ruined and no longer used. Turn right here then immediately left and pass the ruined buildings, bear left at the next fork and right into Birches Road. Cross the stream at the end of the cottages, keep left and cross the second stream by the old pack horse bridge. Turn left when you meet the rough road and follow it into a factory yard. Keep to the right-hand edge of this and you will soon find the riverside path that leads you through to the Jumbles Reservoir. Follow any of the many variations of path that exist until you come to the reservoir side, where a cart track will see you back to your car.

From Hawkshaw to Affetside

This is one of the best bits of the previous walk if you don't want to do the whole lot. It will take about 1¼ hours return, and is best done from Hawkshaw on the Bolton-Burnley road between Bradshaw and Ramsbottom. Park in Hawkshaw Lane between the P.O. and the pub.

Cross the main road and go down a rough cart track straight opposite. Follow this, forking right, until it crosses the outflow over a weir from a small reservoir. On the left, rather inconspicuous, there is a swing gate into a field. The footpath is faint at first, but rapidly improves and becomes a good track contouring the little valley almost to Two Brooks Farm. Then it climbs steeply, goes between two small reservoirs and up through hay fields to the B6213 Tottington road. Cross this road and 50 yards away on the right, another footpath starts and will lead you up by the side of the Pack Horse at Affetside. It seems as if this path only goes to a stylishly re-built farm, but it goes right in front of it and then on by the left-hand corner. Return as you came.

Things of Interest

Jumbles Reservoir is not used as a source of domestic water as are the others above it, but it used to store compensation water for release into Bradshaw Brook as required. The road at Affetside is built on the site of the Roman road that ran from Manchester to Ribchester, but nothing remains of it. The Headless Cross is listed as an Ancient Monument, and the pub, the Pack Horse, is a listed building.

Going down to Hawkshaw, the little reservoir is fringed with forget-me-nots in June and often has great flotillas of tadpoles. A little below it, you will see an isolated chimney on the hillside and perhaps wonder where the mill was situated. The mill was right down on the valley bottom and has been demolished. In the early years of the last century the processing of cotton cloth was done out-of-doors, allowing the sun and the rain to do the work that is now done by chemicals. When steam power came along, soot from the chimney spoiled the cloth, so new chimneys were built high on the hillside to take the soot away. They were connected to the mill boilers by a long complex system of flues, which increased the overall height and therefore the draught.

109

See the notes to Walk No.2.1.

FROM HAWKSHAW TO BULL HILL AND PEEL'S
MONUMENT   WALK NO.2.4

Starting at Hawkshaw this makes a very fine afternoon's walk, but as
it goes through the Army's Firing Range, is subjected to the same
access problem as Walk No.3.1 so read those notes.

Parking at Hawkshaw, which is on the A676 Burnley-Bolton road, is
difficult, but can be managed in Hawkshaw Lane between the post
office and the pub. This is where the walk starts.

Time: about 4 hours.

Follow the lane right up the hill passing a number of attractive stone
farms some of which are listed buildings. When you come to the
T-junction, turn left to Graining Farm. Follow the cart track sharply
round the corner of the building and almost at once you will see a
swing gate on your left. Go through this and the next one, cross the
tiny stream and then at once turn right and follow the stream up the
hill. The path has virtually disappeared, but make diagonally left over
the rough pastures aiming at a group of buildings on the cart track that
runs around the edge of the moor. When you've reached this cart
track by the buildings, turn left, and as soon as you've crossed the
biggish stream that runs under the road, as it is here, strike steeply up
right aiming below the fence of another set of buildings in order to
meet the track from Crowthorn End Farm that goes up Bull Hill. Just
below these buildings turn left on an old paved track. It only lasts a
few yards, ending at a gateway. Go through the gateway, turn right
and follow the wall. The track is scarcely visible here, but at the end of
the wall becomes well marked if very boggy. It leads direct to the top of
Bull Hill. The views from Bull Hill are very fine indeed if it is clear.
See Walk No.3.1 for an indication of what you may see.

From Bull Hill move off roughly south east, that's to say, towards
Bury. There's no path, but it's not bad going. Soon you will see the
Stone on the Site of the Pilgrim's Cross, and after that you will find a
good path which winds its way between the two summits of Harcles
Hill. You, however, are a purist, putting in all the summits, so make a
little diversion to do this. From the top of the second one Peel's
Monument can be seen clearly, and a reasonable track will lead you to
it. The monument has recently been restored (see Walk No.3.3 for
notes about it) and there is a very fine view over the whole of South
Lancashire stretching as far as Kinder Scout on a clear day.

110

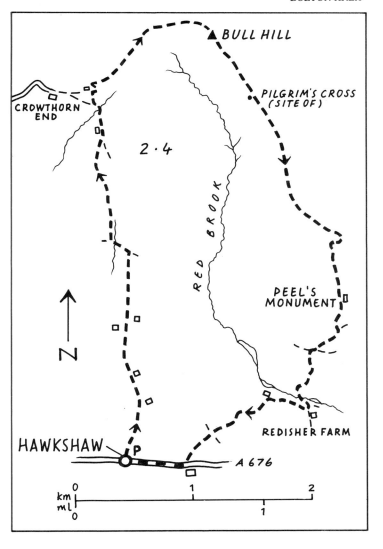

BULL HILL

PILGRIM'S CROSS
(SITE OF)

CROWTHORN
END

2·4

RED BROOK

PEEL'S
MONUMENT

REDISHER FARM

N

HAWKSHAW

P

A 676

| km | 0 | | 1 | | 2 |
| ml | 0 | | | 1 | |

Peel's Monument from Harcles Hill

Leave the monument by the path to Holcombe village but leave it at the end of the wall turning right over a stile. Follow the fence down the steep hillside to the point where it turns sharp left. There take a minor track to the right and cross the stile onto Moorbottom Lane. Go straight across it into the field, go straight down both it and the next one to reach a stile by a War Office notice. Continue straight down the fence but instead of going into the wood at the next stile, bear right and follow the fence down the stream. Cross it easily, turn left and drop down to a wide track. Turn left and follow the next bigger stream for a little way then leave it and climb up to Redisher Farm. Turn right as soon as you are over the stile and turn right again at the farm onto a wide cinder track to Hollingrove Farm.

At the approach to this farm take the diversion track to the left and turn left onto the track that leads to the farm. Follow it to the next house. Turn left into the field just beyond it, (the way is not obvious until you reach the house) and continue to the brook. Here turn right and follow the brook to the next stile then keep going in this direction until you reach a farm access road. Go straight across it through the swing gate and again keep going until you reach the Burnley-Bolton road opposite the mill marked on the 1:25,000 map, SD61/71. Turn right and follow the road until you reach Hawkshaw Lane in about 5 minutes.

Things of Interest

Hawkshaw Lane, at first metalled, then becoming rough and giving agreeable walking, crosses the pastures leading up to the moors, and on it stand a number of fine old farmhouses. In places it runs between bankings crowned with wild rose and hawthorn, and gives good views of the central moors of the Area.

Just before you come to Lower Graining Farm there is a tiny cemetery on your left. It contains just one tombstone, or rather two for the same grave: the original one now cracked and repaired and cracked again, and a modern one side by side. This modern one tells just a little of the story. Roger Worthington was a Baptist minister who died in 1709 aged about 50. He doesn't seem to have been attached to a church, but to have been something of a hermit or a travelling preacher, going amongst the moorland folk who were strong non-conformists, preaching to them. Certainly he must have had a great love of these moors to have been buried alone at the foot of them. See Walk No.3.2 for a note about the Stone on the Site of the Pilgrim's Cross.

A WALK OVER CHETHAM CLOSE, TURTON

WALK NO.2.5

This walk starts at the car park at Turton Tower, which lies just off the B6391 a few hundred yards south of Chapeltown.

Time: about 1½-2 hours.

Return to the wide track that leads to the Tower, turn right and follow it up the little valley to where it ends at a short wall with a gate at either end. Go through the little swing gate to the right onto a wide cart track and follow this until you meet another coming in on your right from Chapeltown. (The mill is directly below.) Here turn left into the field on a rough cart track that soon dwindles to a footpath. At the stile go straight ahead across a patch of very wet ground and climb up to the wood. The path beyond is vague but continue to follow the wall to a fence and stile. Now turn right and follow a well trodden path direct to the Ordnance Survey cairn on top. Chetham Close is 329 metres high, (1,080ft.). It is not quite as high as Turton Heights, (335 metres or 1,100ft.). A few yards away to the right are the remains of two stone circles. Very little indeed remains, but they're worth a look.

Continue following the path across the first wall to a white painted iron stump. Here you join a path that comes up from Egerton. Turn right, and follow it for a few minutes until it starts to swing left.

113

The Railway Bridge

Instead, keep straight on. There's a bit of path to follow. Go through a gap in the wall and aim at the long wall running downhill on your right. There's a stile in the fence at the bottom that brings you onto the metalled road leading to Clough House Farm. Follow it past the farm and past the track leading up from the mill that you used to start the walk. Then when this cart track goes through a gate to join another cart track, turn left, and a few more minutes brings you back over the railway to Turton Tower. This railway bridge is an interesting architectural curiosity, built in the style of a Norman castle.

WAYOH AND THE BROADHEAD VALLEY   WALK NO.2.6

This walk covers some very varied countryside along the upper part of the Wayoh Reservoir and up the north-east side of the Broadhead Valley to Lower House. The first part of the return across the valley is not easy to follow, and this return is only recommended if you are experienced in following disused footpaths.

Time: 3 hours or 1½ hours if you only go to look at the old coke ovens.

The walk is best started from the new car park at Entwistle Reservoir. To find this, see Walk No.2.1.2. Walk across the reservoir embankment and take the wide rough road on the right. Bear left in front of the pub, then right cross the railway and a little way down the road go over a stile on the left. Go diagonally left into the wood then keeping left go through the wood to find a stile almost at its end. Now go up almost to a pond and bear right to a stile and bridge over the stream. Now follow this path up to Wayoh Fold Farm. As you approach the farm make for the gate to the left of the buildings and go straight ahead on the farm track, past a barn of unusual design, onto the road. Turn left up the road, and about 50 yards away you will see a footpath signpost. Take this track up to Naze End, staying on the upper one when it forks. Follow this upper track until it has climbed to the top of the moor. Then straight ahead, some 2-300 yards away you will see the group of beehive-type coke ovens. Keep straight on through a stile by a gate - beware of an electric fence - then make across the wet moor to them. There are seven in all, arranged in two rows. They are built of local stone burnt red and partially melted by the great heat developed - a most surprising sight, for there are no obvious remains of coal mining. From them drop straight down through a gap in the wall to the cart track below.

If you now wish to return to you car turn right and retrace your steps as far as the head of Wayoh from where you may take a different route back to your car. See Walk No.2.1.2 short return.

Otherwise follow the cart track up the valley to the next farm, Lower House, also deserted. Here at the end of the buildings there is a stile in the trees and a path goes down the field to a stile to the river. The bridge has completely gone, but you won't find any difficulty in crossing a few yards above it.

Follow a faint path up the field until you are opposite some farm buildings. Then you will see a good bridge below you on the right. Cross it and make upwards and right to a clump of hawthorns just ahead that hide some ruined buildings. Now comes the only difficult bit, getting to Orrell's Farm. Keep to the right of the hawthorns but bear left before you come to a pair of stone gate posts. You will pass between the large group of thorns and another smaller one to your right. Just beyond you will see a straight deep cut hollow, once the access road to the ruined farm which is now hidden in the bushes and overgrown with grass. Follow its right bank and where it ends keep straight on going through a pair of gate posts then through a purpose made gap in the wire fence. The very faint path you have been following now disappears or goes up the hill. You just keep straight on aiming at the farm ahead, Orrell's Farm. You have to cross a deep cut valley where you will find a good bridge, and as you climb out of it you will find a grassy or often muddy cart track leading you past the farm onto its access road. Follow this cart track back to the road. Turn right and then left in about 50 yards to Moorside Farm. Go left between the farm and the barn to find the stile into the field and follow this path to Hill Top Farm. Go through the elegant forecourt of the house through the side gate onto the lane. Follow the lane turning right at the junction just crossing the road into Hob Lane. Follow it to the upper dam of Wayoh Reservoir and return to your car by Walk No.2.1.2.

Things of Interest
The banks of the upper arm of the Wayoh Reservoir support a good selection of wild flowers. See Walk No.2.1 for a list of some of them. The Broadhead Valley's name describes its appearance exactly. When you have crossed the valley to Orrell's Farm, look back and you will see that the moorland on the side of the valley you have just left extends considerably lower down the sides of the valley than on the side where you are now walking. The reason for this is that it faces the prevailing wind and gets a heavier rainfall, and when this exceeds about 50-60 inches per annum, moorland overtakes pasture. The things of greatest interest in this walk are the beehive coke ovens above Naze End. They are of the earliest type and it is possible that they were built as long ago as 1800. It is known that Abraham Darby was using coke to smelt iron in his Coalbrookdale furnace as early as 1708. There are the scant remains of iron smelting across the valley in the Army's land. It is possible that coke was made here for use across the valley for coal was mined on the spot as well as a little higher up the valley. There are still fragments of coal and coke around.

FROM HORROCKS FOLD TO BELMONT BY
    LONGWORTH CLOUGH   WALK NO.2.7

The start of this walk isn't really up to standard, but the finishing part is excellent. In many ways it would be just as well to start near Higher Critchley Fold, but how do you get back there from Belmont except rather drearily along the road? At least by starting at Horrocks Fold you can come back on the bus. They are rather infrequent, so ring Manchester 226-8181 for their times and allow 2½ hours for the walk. (If you decide to start near Higher Critchley Fold, take the Belmont road from Egerton. The cinder track starts as soon as the road has

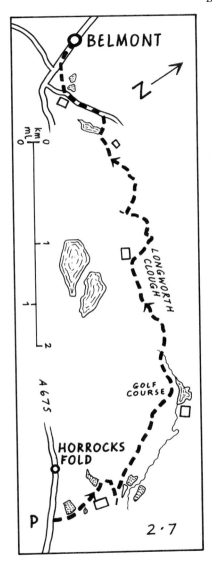

BELMONT

km
ml.
0
0

1

1

2

LONGWORTH CLOUGH

A 675

GOLF
COURSE

HORROCKS
FOLD

P

2·7

crossed the brook and joins the main walk at the bridge over Eagley Brook.)

Starting from Horrocks Fold, take the A675 out of Bolton, until soon after passing Sweetloves Reservoir, houses on the right come to an abrupt end. Turn right at the end of them and park. Go straight on and continue on the gravel track past the works to a house and then by a field path to one of the dozens of small mill reservoirs in this part of Bolton. From the corner of the reservoir cut across by a tip to a cinder track to the right. Follow this to it first fork, turn left, and keep left when another cinder track comes in from the right. You now join a bit of tarmac but not for long. It goes up the hill to the Golf Club, you go right along a wide cinder track. It's walled, thick with blackberry, and divides Dunscar golf course into two. Then it descends gently to Eagley Brook. Cross the bridge and go straight on up the brookside, rich with flowers in spring and summer, to the paper mill.

The way through the mill buildings is as follows: As you enter the complex, follow the tarmac until it turns sharp left. There keep straight on, up a bit of old cobbled path and some steps to a storage area slightly on your right. Go through this area, and when the road forks, take the right-hand branch which will take you out of the mill area and on to a farm. Immediately past the farm there is the remains of a swing gate on the right. Go through this. The track is faint, but aim just to the right of the iron gate where you will find the water leat. Follow the leat right round the curve of Longworth Clough, whose woods and stream can be well seen from this high level and unusual path. Go beyond the round gurgling pond of Belmont Sewage Works to the Ornamental Reservoir where you may disturb the heron and ducks. Turn right across the dam, go over the bridge and straight up the field to a stile in the corner by a tree. This is often a hay field and the track barely visible. Keep in single file. If you are walking back to Higher Critchely Fold, turn right here. Otherwise turn left and follow the road down to the works of the Belmont Dyeing and Bleaching Co. Take a short cut by their visitors' car park direct to Maria Square and the bus stop, Belmont. You should have time for a look around this spot.

Things of Interest
Longworth Clough is famous for its flowers, and there are several sites of special interest to botanists. In the marshy woods below the paper mill you can see marsh marigolds, mayflowers, bistort, Himalayan balsam, meadow sweet, and one fairly rare one - pink purselane.

The water leat is another good place for moisture loving plants.

There you may find the common valerian, not so common round here. Towards its end the leat is becoming choked with plants and reeds. This is really pond sedge. There's a much better known sedge in the Ornamental Reservoir - the bulrush. The woods in the upper part of the clough contain many rowans and are carpeted with bilberry in places.

Belmont Village has one of the finest situations in the whole of the Area. Whilst not a moorland village, it is much influenced by them. You will find the best views of it from the east, around Higher Whittacker, for example. There are a number of listed buildings in the main street of which Maria Square, built in 1804 is perhaps the best example. On the opposite corner from its distinctive name plate is an old 'Sabbath School' built in 1832. Originally in cut stone like the rest of the square, it has been heavily rendered at some time, losing character. A further item of interest in this corner is the granite obelisk commemorating the struggle that the residents of Belmont had to gain 'rights for all time and to perpetuity' of compensation water from the Belmont Reservoir when it was taken over by Bolton Corporation in 1907. It was quite an affair judging by the inscription. Across the road, opposite the Black Dog, is one of the many drinking fountains and troughs erected to celebrate Queen Victoria's Diamond Jubilee. Today the water no longer flows and the trough is planted with flowers.

BARROW BRIDGE, DEAN BROOK AND RIVINGTON PIKE
WALK NO.2.8

Barrow Bridge is a beauty spot known to the people of Bolton for many years. It used to have a tea-room; today it has a car park and picnic place and is a Conservation Area. No one would think that Barrow Bridge was once a thriving industrial village. To read more about it, turn to Barrow Bridge in the chapter on conservation areas.

The walk to the Pike is quite long but the walk up Dean Brook only takes an hour there and back.

It's best to get to Barrow Bridge by leaving the Moss Bank Way ring road, A58 at Moss Bank Park and generally keeping left until you come to Barrow Bridge. The car park is on the left at the end of the village. There is also a bus service from Bolton.

The Short Walk
If you have arrived by bus go on up the road passing the car park in a

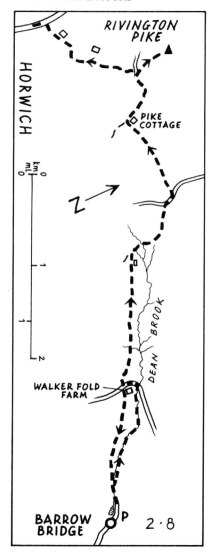

few hundred yards. There are some fine old houses both at the road side and across the water leat, a feature of the place. If you have arrived by car the car park is beyond these houses. Continue the length of the road until it turns sharp right, uphill. At the end is a path leading to a set of steps, at the foot of which, on the right is a stile. This is the start of the footpath up Dean Brook, a delightful wooded clough. After the first bridge the path splits several times. Always take the one nearest to the stream. You will have to cross and re-cross several times; no problem in summer but in a wet spell it could be difficult in shoes. Eventually you will find one rough path at water level in quite a deep cut part of the stream, a miniature gorge. There's no need to cross again until the very end, just before you reach the road at Walker Fold Farm. Then it's easy.

Here, if time is short, go left up the hill to the farm where there is a footpath marked by a finger post that leads quickly and directly back to Barrow Bridge. If you have a little more time you may prefer to turn right up the road, go past Colliers Row to the lane opposite the old school. Turn down this and you will be back in Barrow Bridge within 10 or 15 minutes.

The Long Walk

If you have a whole afternoon to spare this extends the previous walk to include some good moorland walking and some of the best views in the Area - if it's clear. In fact, it's one of the best walks. It is easier to use public transport: bus to Barrow Bridge from Bolton, and bus back to Bolton from Horwich.

Go to Walker Fold Farm as just described. Turn left on the road and just past the farm a finger post directs you to the required footpath on the right. It may be very wet to start, but eventually improves with a row of paving stones down the middle. It ends at the former Burnt Edge Colliery, and a few yards higher up the hillside another track comes slanting in from the left. Go up to it, and follow it up the rest of the valley. At the valley head it curves gently right and crosses a little stream. Within 50 or 60 yards a wall comes in on the left and a path branches off and runs up besides it. Follow this track until it reaches the metalled road leading to the T.V. mast on Winter Hill. (From here it is possible to reverse route 1.14.) Turn right and after about 100 yards a track leads off on the left, passes a water intake, and goes down to the upper part of Georges Lane. (If you want to go up Winter Hill as well, keep on the metalled road all the way. See Walk No.1.5 for some guidance.) Follow Georges Lane to the foot of the Pike, climb it and enjoy the views. The quickest way back to Horwich is to return down Georges Lane to a big clump of rhododendrons. Just before you get there, there is a swing gate on the right leading to a grassy cart track that runs down to Higher Knoll Farm. From there it's concreted, and takes you down to the rough lane behind Rivington School. Turn left and left again onto Lever Park Avenue, and you will find the bus stop at the end of it by the main road.

Whilst you are on the Pike you are very close to the Ornamental Gardens. Have a look there if you've time. The rough road that divides them in two will take you down to the Rivington School. Allow about half an hour to the bus stop. See the 'Things of Interest' section

Dean Brook and Barrow Bridge

for walks in Section One for a description of the Pike, the Ornamental Gardens and Lever Park.

Things of Interest

Dean Brook Wood is typical of the wooded cloughs on the western edge of the moors. It is mainly oak with some birch, sycamore, and alder by the brook and is carpeted with bluebells in the spring. Across the top the upper part has been planted with spruce and beech, and is not really in character.

Colliers Row originally housed the colliers who worked at the former Burnt Edge Colliery about a mile further up the brook. The school further along Scout Road was built to educate their children. It is now a Grade 2 listed building. Behind Colliers Row is Brownstones Quarry, much used by local climbers as a practice ground. It was one of the first quarries in Britain to be used for climbing.

3. WALKS AROUND HELMSHORE, HASLINGDEN AND HOLCOMBE

ASCENTS OF BULL HILL

As Bull Hill is the highest point (418 metres, 1,372ft.) in the eastern section of the Area, and is second only to Winter Hill (456 metres, 1,498ft.) in the whole Area its ascent deserves pride of place in this section. It is, however, somewhat bedevilled by the Army's firing ranges. The area of land used by the Army is outlined on the map with the words 'Danger Area' and is liberally marked on the ground with notice boards stating, 'Keep out when the red flag is flying'. At present the Army uses eight flags in prominent positions around its boundaries to indicate when firing is in progress and flags are only flown during that period. A ring of posts has now been erected around the danger area to define it more closely. The Army does not use the firing range every day, does not fire after 3.00 p.m. on Sundays nor after 5.00 p.m. on weekdays. Ring the Liaison Officer at Holcombe Moor Camp, Tottington 2991, in normal office hours to ascertain the orders for the day you are interested in. He will try to help you if he can.

In 1984 the Army acquired an additional piece of land between the moor and their range in Holcombe Head. Walk No.3.3 passes through it. Besides firing practice on the range they now use the whole area for what is called 'dry training', when troops on exercises use blanks, not live ammunition. Walkers may well come across troops on these exercises. They should know that all soldiers operating in the area will have been briefed as to the public's rights there. An officer may possibly ask them to wait a few minutes before continuing or to make a small diversion to their route.

During 1986 the Ministry of Defence made proposals to acquire a further large portion of land on Holcombe Moor. It would include the whole of Harcles Hill and Peel's Monument and would be used to extend the 'dry training' area. The Army state categorically that they do not intend to close any public or other footpaths in this area. A number of amenity bodies have objected as have local residents and some individuals. The outcome is not known as planning permission is required and has not yet been granted.

The path from the B6214 Haslingden-Bury old road is the shortest way. It starts close to Buckden Wood, the only expanse of woodland on both sides of the road round here. Unfortunately it's not named on the map, though Lower Buckden Farm is and this gives you some guidance. There is a lay-by for parking on the west side of the road by the wood.

Time: 30 minutes to the top, 50 minutes return, or 2 hours for the

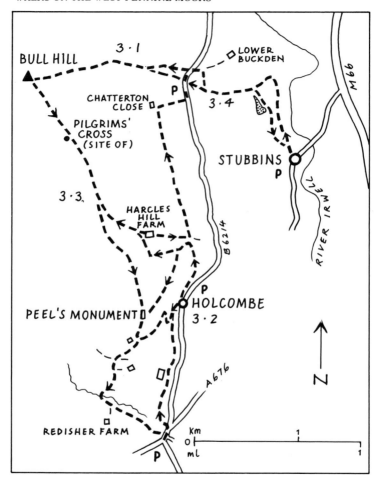

longer trip.

Take the cart track up the field marked by a signpost. At the next gate go straight ahead, fairly steeply to start, passing old mine spoil heaps on your right. It then runs more easily to the top of Bull Hill. Return as you came, or, if you prefer, extend the walk past the site of

Bull Hill and Harcles Hill

the Pilgrim's Cross and go down to Harcles Hill Farm by the track from there. At Harcles Hill Farm follow their road down the hill until it meets the cart track that runs all the way from near the White Horse, Helmshore, to Holcombe. Turn left on this track, not very clear in parts, until you come to Chatterton Close. Opposite the farm turn right down a lane that will bring you to the road and to your car in a couple of minutes.

If, however it is more convenient to start from the Bolton side of the hill, get to the road end above Crowthorn Reservoir by turning off the B6232 Blackburn-Haslingden road opposite the Grey Mare, following it to Crowthorn and then turning left, or from Bolton via Bradshaw and Edgworth.

Time: 50 minutes return.

There is room to park off the road just past the white house of Crowthorn End. Then walk up the upper bit of tarmac road and just before it reaches the heavily fenced agricultural buildings, turn left on an old paved track. It only lasts a few yards, ending at a gateway. Go through the gateway, turn right and follow the wall. The track is scarcely visible here, but at the end of the wall becomes well marked if very boggy. It leads directly to the top of Bull Hill.

If you are using public transport, it is best to climb Bull Hill from Stubbins. Turn to Walk No.3.4 to see how to start. When you reach the road after the first part of the wood, turn right and in about 100 yards you will see the finger post indicating the start of the walk just described.

Peel's Monument

A VISIT TO PEEL'S MONUMENT, HOLCOMBE

WALK NO.3.2

The monument stands stark on the skyline just above Holcombe. It was built in 1852 to honour Bury's most famous son, Sir Robert Peel, born in 1788. It was built by public subscription from local stone and is 120ft. high. It became unsafe during the War and its entrance was bricked up but has now been restored and is open to the public again. On a clear day the whole of South Lancashire and further afield can be seen from the top. Manchester's tower blocks stand out clearly and the dish of the radio telescope at Jodrell Bank is easily seen. The hills of the Peak District make a backcloth to that view. Further right Frodsham and Helsby hills stand out quite boldly and beyond them the mountains of North Wales.

Peel's claim to fame is twofold. He was Prime Minister of the government that repealed the Corn Laws. These laws were enacted between 1789 and 1815 to require the payment of duty on imported corn. This made the price of bread artificially high and caused great hardship amongst Lancashire cotton operatives who understandably were more than grateful for their repeal. He was also the founder of the police force.

To find Holcombe get onto the B6214, the Haslingden-Bury old road at the road junction at Holcombe Brook. Holcombe village is a short mile up the road. Parking is difficult, but the Lancashire C.C. hope to provide some in due course. Meanwhile, you can but use the Shoulder of Mutton's car park and hope for the best.

The shortest way for a quick visit will take you only about 30 minutes return from the Shoulder of Mutton at Holcombe, itself a delightful corner partly on a bridleway below the moor.

Across the road from the pub, well to the left, you will see a telephone kiosk. Turn left on the bridle track here, turn right at the first junction, then left at the next one. The track zig-zags its way up in an obvious manner. Return as you came, or take small variations as the many tracks allow.

A much easier but longer way is to start as for the visit to the Pilgrim's Cross (Walk No.3.3), but before reaching the quarries, turn left along the back of a wall. This track now runs more or less direct to the monument. If you wish to make the round trip, allow about 45 minutes.

Within the illustration:
ON THIS SITE
STOOD THE ANCIENT
PILGRIM'S CROSS
IT WAS EXISTING
A.D. 1176
AND PERHAPS MUCH
EARLIER
PILGRIMS TO WHALLEY
ABBEY PRAYED AND
RESTED HERE

TO THE SITE OF THE PILGRIM'S CROSS AND
PEEL'S MONUMENT   WALK NO.3.3

The site is on a very old track running between Bull Hill and Harcles Hill, but this track is now indistinct through lack of use and is difficult to find. Nowadays there is a good track from Harcles Hill Farm, though it is not a right of way.

This walk takes a much longer route than the previous one as it starts in Holcombe Brook and returns by Redisher Woods. The path along the moor goes through the 'Danger Area'. See the notes to Walk No.3.1.

Time: 2½ hours.

There is a car park in Longsight road, B6214 close to its junction with the Bolton-Burnley road, the A676. Cross the A676 and turn right. Immediately above the Hare and Hounds turn left into a wide rough road and then right up a signed bridleway in about 100 yards. This is the former coach road between Bury and Haslingden. Follow it climbing gently all the time passing the former Aitkin Sanatorium, now an Islamic Training Centre, and the Manor House, a fine three storey stone-built house. Go to the left of the house when you meet the road and you will pass a picturesque house with an iron balcony, High House.

Follow this road, climbing all the time, to the old school and the start of a cart track that goes up to the old quarries near Harcles Hill Farm. Follow this track until you are as high as the top wall of the farm enclosure. Cut across to the wall and go behind it past the farm buildings until you join the track coming up from the farm. Then follow this unmistakably to the site of the cross.

Peel's Monument is out of sight but a well-trodden track goes to the right of Harcles Hill directly to it. Leave the Momument by the path to Holcombe village but leave this at the end of the wall, turning right over a stile. Follow the fence down the steep hillside to the point where it turns sharp left. There turn right on a minor track and cross the stile onto Moorbottom Lane. Go straight across it into the field, go straight down both it and the next one to reach a stile by a War Office notice. Continue straight down the fence but instead of going into the wood at the next stile, bear right and follow the fence down to the stream. Cross it easily, turn left and drop down onto a wide track. Turn left and follow the main stream for a little way, then leave it and climb up to Redisher Farm just visible above the wood. Bear left here and continue along a well-trodden track along the top of the wood to the main road. Your car is round the corner of the crossroads.

The Pilgrim's Cross stood on one of the long lost tracks of Norman England. Its origins are lost in the mists of antiquity, and there seems to be no record of when it was placed there or when it was lost. However, there is a record that pilgrims travelling to Whalley Abbey rested and prayed there. The present stone was placed on the site on May 4th 1904, by the copyholders of the Manor of Holcombe and other interested people.

Holcombe village is of ancient origin going back to at least the thirteenth century, but most of today's buildings date from the 17th and 18th centuries when farming was supplemented by handloom weaving so increasing the area's prosperity. Hey House which is passed on the return is dated 1616 and is a very fine house, unfortunately hidden from view.

FROM STUBBINS ROUND BUCKDEN WOODS
WALK NO.3.4

Buckden Woods are National Trust property and make a delightful walk, but it is difficult to make a satisfactory round trip. Stubbins is on the A56 between Ramsbottom and Rawtenstall. Park in a side street or at the Railway Hotel, which as its name suggests, is close to the railway bridge. Public transport will also get you there.

Time: 1-1¼ hours.

From the Railway Hotel go under the railway and turn right. The road leads into Stubbins Vale Works, but it is also a footpath that leads right through. Follow it until it meets the railway, the old dismanted Helmshore line, but do not go under the bridge. Keep on the left-hand side and the road soon becomes a cart track and the cart track a footpath that leads into the woods. At first there is only one way to go, but higher up the path forks. Take the right-hand one, cross the brook by a huge stone slab - take care when it's wet - and re-cross about 70-80 yards higher up. This time there's no bridge, but it is not difficult. Now the path climbs on the left quite steeply and soon emerges on the road by a stile. You can cross the road and enter the upper part of the wood, also a National Trust property. The paths here are very thready and difficult to follow up the steep watercourse, and it's not nearly so enjoyable as the lower part. Eventually you can scramble out by a stile at the top close to where the footpath leads from the road to Bull Hill. Descend to the road by that path.

Go straight across the road down the lane that leads to Lower Buckden Farm. Very soon you will come to a branch on the right that passes a barn and leads down to the woods again. Follow the track down, reversing the route you came up, until you come in sight of a small stone house on the right of the brook. Take the path towards it. It leads into a lane that goes past a small reservoir and overlooks a mill. Turn left at the first house you come to and very quickly you will be on the road to the mill where you started.

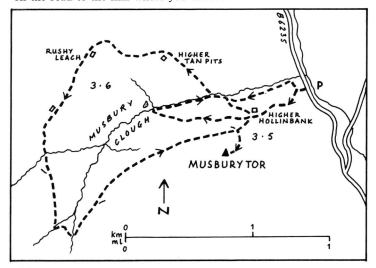

Musbury Tor from High Hollingbank

THE ASCENT OF MUSBURY TOR   WALK NO.3.5

Musbury Tor is a steep sided, flat topped hill only 1,114ft. (338 metres) high. It is fringed with rocks on three sides and looks quite impressive.

Park on a small piece of open ground opposite Household Textiles, Holcombe Road, Helmshore. This is the B6235 and it links the B6232 and the B6215 road on the south-west side of Haslingden. Alternatively park at the Museum of the Lancashire Textile Industry, formerly known as Higher Mill Museum, about 200 yards away on the same road. In this case turn left when you leave the car park and walk about 200 yards along the road to find the open ground mentioned above.

Time: about ¾ hour return.

Walk up the walled path that leaves on the left of a solitary house and leads to Higher Hollinbank. At this house go through the swing gate into the yard and across the yard into the field below the wall. Do not go through the gate that seems to lead directly to the Tor. Keep below the wall, and turn left with it when it swings up the hill. Where

133

it meets the next wall you will find a stile, and over this a track slanting up left and climbing quite gently leads to the top. Views over Haslingden and up the Rossendale Valley are very good, and if it is clear, you can see Ingleborough and Penyghent. It's a particularly worthwhile walk late in the evening when all the streep lamps are lit and the Valley spread at your feet in a pattern of coloured lights. Return as you came.

TWO WALKS AROUND MUSBURY CLOUGH
WALK NO.3.6

Musbury Clough is overlooked by the Tor and is one of the nicest spots on the eastern side of the Recreational Area. It has trees, a little lake, a trout stream and some deep-cut hollows climbing steeply up to the moor. Both walks start at the same place, one is quite short taking only 30-40 minutes, the other about 1½ hours.

See the previous walk for approaches and parking places. Leave the one opposite Household Textiles at the back, turning right across the bridge onto a cinder track. Opposite some cottages go through a gate on the left. Be careful to shut it and the next one as this is grazing land. This track meets a walled lane going sharply left by a row of cottages. The shorter walk goes left up the walled lane and the longer one goes straight ahead across the stream.

For the short walk, follow the walled lane to Higher Hollinbank. Here, on the right, there are two gates in a corner. Go through the lower one and follow the wall until it turns up the hill. Then keep straight on, neither climbing nor descending, until the path becomes clear. Then it drops gently to the brook. Cross the brook by a little bridge, climb the wall by the stile, turn right and follow the path back to your car. You can do this walk the other way round but it is probably easier to find the paths this way. It is also possible to climb the Tor whilst you are up at Higher Hollinbank. See Walk No.3.5 for the details, and allow an extra 30 minutes.

For the longer walk follow the stream for about 100 yards to a stile and a walled lane on the right. Turn right into the lane. This lane passes a NWWA water intake and goes up to the ruins of Higher Tan Pits Farm. Go past the ruins on the right, staying in the walled lane which ends at an extremely awkward stile. Struggle over it and continue along a well-trodden grassy track that gives good views up the valley until you come to the second of two marker posts. It is close to a wall with a gap in it. These posts mark the route of the Rossendale

Way, but you are not following it on this walk. The post, however, does mark the point at which you will find the path that runs right round the valley head. Turn left on it. Here it is quite well-trodden but after the next ruin, Rushy Leach, you have to follow the line of a slight ridge which brings you easily to the next ruin. Leave it by the gateway on the left and follow a well-trodden path through a gateway, cross a stream above a delightful waterfall and climb up to another track that runs round the valley head. After crossing two major streams climb gently up to the top wall, but do not cross the stile there. It leads to Gt. House Farm. Instead, walk along neither climbing nor descending for a little way until you find a path that leads below the rocks of the Tor. Follow this above the wall until you come to the stile. Go over it, follow the wall turning right when it turns, until it brings you into the lane at Higher Hollinbank. Turn left and 5 minutes will see you back to your car.

Things of Interest

Musbury Clough was the site of a medieval deer park. It reached up to the moor, across into the next clough, Alden Clough, and over to where Holden Wood Reservoir is situated today. The deer were kept in by a ditch and an earth bank topped by a stout paling fence. There are said to be traces left but there is good documentary evidence for the boundaries, and for other deer parks within the Area. This deer park was created by the Lords of Clitheroe in 1304 A.D. in order to retain and conserve deer for their hunting pleasures. These pleasures didn't last long for in 1322 A.D. the King confiscated it because of acts of treason by Thomas of Lancaster at the Battle of Borough Bridge. In 1408 A.D. it was no longer a hunting ground and was carved up into lots and sold in 1507 A.D. Two hundred and fifty years later the valley housed a dozen small farms. The people kept a few cows and sheep, but their principal source of income was handloom weaving using local wool. At the turn of the eighteenth century water powered spinning mills were developed and one at least was situated just behind the row of cottages where this walk starts. Nothing remains except the outlines of its mill ponds, easily seen from the short walk which passes above them. The little lake further up the valley conserved water for these mills and today its water is sent through to the Grane Reservoir.

In spring, moorland birds, the curlew and lapwing especially, are often seen in the higher parts of the valley. Sometimes there's a carrion crow. In the trees, thrushes, blackbirds and chaffinches abound. Pied wagtails can be seen by the stream.

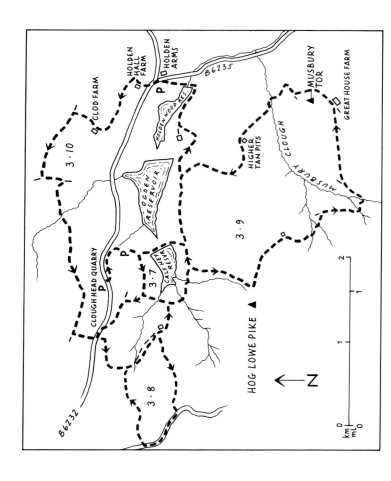

THE CALF HEY TRAIL

Access and Parking

The Calf Hey Trail seems to be the brain-child of the Rossendale Groundwork Trust which has been establised to promote improvements to the landscape and increase opportunities for countryside recreation. It has been implemented by the Lancashire County Council with contributions from the NWWA and grant-aided by the Countryside Commission. The Trail is about 2 miles beyond Heap Clough on the Haslingden-Blackburn road, B6232, travelling from Haslingden. The entrance to its car park is well marked when travelling in this direction but it is not at all easily seen when travelling from Blackburn, despite advance notices.

This car park is quite small and it is evidently intended that use should be made of the Clough Head Quarry car park and picnic site on the opposite side of the road and easily spotted when travelling from Blackburn. This car park and picnic site is a fine example of land reclamation. The derelict quarry has been landscaped, re-seeded, and small trees planted. In a few years time this will be a well sheltered picnic site, hopefully with toilets. To find the Calf Hey Trail from it, leave by the swing gate near the entrance. A newly made footpath takes you to the road. Cross it at that point; lower down there is less visibility and traffic moves at speed. Great care is needed with children. About 50 yards lower down the footpath starts again and brings you in about 5 minutes to the road leading to the other car park. There's no need to use it though. Straight opposite, a stile and path take you there.

Time to walk the Trail: about an hour. It is suitable for shoes in dry weather.

Leave the Calf Hey car park by the obvious gate and continue along the wide cart track to marker post 3. You will pass the ruins of Hartley House (being excavated during the summer of 1986). At marker post 3 keep straight on for a few yards to find the ruins of Lower Ormerods, already freed from rubble and grass so that you can see the lay-out of the rooms. There are stone steps, fireplaces, even cupboards, for stone was the local building material. From the marker post cross the stream and carry on up the steps. (Here a shorter and less interesting route goes along the reservoir bank to join the main trail a little further on,) The Trail continues across the base of Hog Lowe Clough where there is a fragment of ancient woodland, oak, ash, rowan, alder and willow, a very pleasant spot. Much of the woodland around the reservoir is conifer, some of it planted by the Forestry Commission in the 1960's

137

to investigate the effects of air pollution on tree growth. A weir has been built across the big stream from Hog Lowe Clough to trap stones and it is worth noting that the water does not flow directly into the reservoir but into a channel alongside it from which it can be turned either into Calf Hey or Ogden reservoir lower down the valley. The Trail leads you back to the reservoir banks and to the dam which you cross. Climb up to the stile and turn right to find the car park.

Extension to the Calf Hey Trail

This extension takes you round the head of the valley and is a very much shortened version of Walk No.3.10 and offers some of the fine views of the valley that that walk has. It will take an extra hour and light boots are strongly recommended.

At Hartley House (marker post 2) leave the Trail and bear right a little onto the path that follows the wall to Ormerods. Just after this ruin cross a stile to the right and shortly afterwards you will find yourself in a stony walled lane. It leads you into another lane where you turn left and follow the wide now grassy track to a stile onto the road. Now turn left and about 50 yards up the road go back into the field by another stile. You have now joined Walk No.3.10 which you follow to marker post 5.

Here you have a choice of routes:
1. Follow the Trail back to the car park.
2. Continue to follow Walk No.3.10 as far as the solitary tree by the fence. Here a stile on the left will put you on a path straight down to the dam and the Calf Hey Trail.

Things of Interest

The Calf Hey Trail gives you not just a walk round the reservoir but gives you a look into a valley which though now almost empty of houses was once the home of around 1,000 people. Until 1507 it was part of the Musbury Deer Park. Then the forest laws that preserved the park as the hunting ground of noblemen were abolished. Up to that time much of the land was woodland. It was gradually cut down so that people could settle and farm the land, a process that went on for the next 200 years. Their grazing animals prevented re-generation of the woodland which only survived in a few inaccessible places like Hog Lowe Clough. Slowly the community there increased and 150 years ago over a thousand people earned a living there by farming, handloom weaving and the surreptitious whisky distilling, known as 'whisky spinning'. The community had a chapel and graveyard, still to be seen today. It is best approached from the near end of the car park going down a flight of steps to a tiny picnic area and then turning left. Here you will see old gravestones dated 1820-30 and a modern one stating that here was the site of the Methodist Chapel of the village of Haslingden Grane, built in 1815 and demolished in 1955. There is another similar graveyard by the side of the main road, just below the lane where you started. Here a cross carries a plate inscribed to the effect that this is where the Church of St. Stephen, parish church of Haslingden Grane, used to stand. It was pulled down and re-erected stone by stone on a site 1½ miles nearer Haslingden and re-consecrated in 1927.

Haslingden Grane continued as a community even after Calf Hey Reservoir was built between 1854 and 1859 to supply Bury and Ratcliffe with drinking water. It slowly lost its population as British agriculture fell on hard times in the 1880s and by the time the Ogden Reservoir was built in 1912 the upper part of the valley was deserted. Holden Wood Reservoir was built in 1841 to supply compensation water to the mills in the valley below.

A WALK TO PICKUP BANK HEIGHTS FROM
CALF HEY RESERVOIR   WALK NO.3.8

In effect this is an extension to the extension of the previous walk but done the other way round. Pickup Bank Heights forms the western boundary of the Grane Recreational Management Zone and it has very good views of the Darwen Moors. Route finding is not very easy as it wanders amongst the former fields, now reverted to rough grazing, of the Grane farms.

Start by following the Calf Hey Trail as far as marker post 5. Pass the pair of gate posts, making for a solitary one a little way ahead and continue in the same direction. You will pick up a well-trodden grassy track that winds its way up the hill passing another pair of gate posts and arrive at the top corner of the wood. Cross the stile here, turn right and go down to the ruins of Top o'th'Knoll.

A few yards beyond the farm leave the lane on the left through a convenient gap in the wall climbing steeply up making for a small hawthorn tree by a wall. The path is faint and continues faintly in the same direction to the next wall corner. Now turn right and continue across this field until you come to a locked gate and stile on your left. Go over the stile and follow the old quarry track keeping straight ahead at a sort of crossroads and you will find yourself on the tarmac at Pickup Bank Heights. Turn right and follow the road for 7 or 8 minutes. There are good views of Darwen Tower out to your left, even better if you leave the road for the steep escarpment on your left.

When you have passed some old quarry spoil heaps keep a look out for a cart track going off on the right. It becomes a walled lane, but it is easier to follow the tractor marks to the right. They will bring you to a stile which you cross and then you follow first the wall then the wire fence on your left to stay on this track until you enter a field. Now all traces of this well-marked track disappear. Turn right and follow the wall down the hillside. A track gradually appears and strengthens - it is not a right of way track - that was further to the right, but has utterly disappeared. This way at least, you can follow without too much difficulty. This track will eventually join another cart track and the two of them become very well-marked taking you to a locked gate onto the road. To find the stile you must bear left about 100 yards before you reach this gate.

Now walk down the road all of 50 yards to a good stile and finger post on the right. Cross over onto an excellent green track and follow this back to Calf Hey. It has fine views of Hog Lowe Pike and the whole of the upper Grane Valley.

HOG LOWE PIKE AND THE ROUND OF MUSBURY
WALK NO.3.9

This very fine walk has some hard going and boots are strongly recommended. Views are exceptionally fine and varied if it is done this way round.

Time: about 3½ hours.

Park at the Clough Head car park, Haslingden Grane, on the B6231 road and follow the path to the Calf Hey car park. See the previous Walk for instructions. Now go through the gate and cross the dam of Calf Hey Reservoir. Continue straight ahead on a faint path to a stile close to a solitary tree. Turn right on a well-marked path and follow it along the hillside to the junction with the Calf Hey Trail on the edge of Hog Lowe Clough. Turn left up the clough following the fence at first, then more steeply up the flank of the clough. Almost at the top of the clough the path crosses over to a stile (ignore an earlier one on the left) and Hog Lowe Pike comes into view almost at once. Follow the grassy path to it and enjoy the wide view. Winter Hill with its TV and other masts lies straight ahead and Darwen Tower is perched on the end of the moor to its right. Behind you there is Pendle Hill with Boulsworth on its right. Cribden, which overlooks Haslingden, is in

Hog Lowe Pike

front of it and the flat top of Whitworth Moor is prominent to its right.

Face the direction from which you have come and follow first the fence and then the wall to its first corner. The path now becomes faint but goes diagonally right and brings you over the moor to the ruins of Causeway End, out of sight below the wall. Here it is possible to shorten the walk by an hour or so if you wish, cutting out the fine circuit of the Musbury Valley. (See below for these instructions.) Otherwise follow a faint path towards the head of the valley. It just keeps its height to start with, drops down to cross a stream and then follows a wall to join the main path around the valley head. Turn left on this and follow it right round the valley, crossing two major streams on the way. Now climb up gently to the right to a stile into a green field, a strange sight on the top of the moor and an example of what can be done to rough moorland grazing, and follow the track down to Great House Farm. Turn left in front of the gate leading into it and follow the wall to a stile. After the second stile bear left to find the gate into Higher Hollinbank's yard. It is out of sight in a corner.

Leave the yard by a walled lane on your left and turn left as soon as you have passed the row of cottages. At the end of the open space turn right into a rough walled lane and follow it up to the ruins of Higher Tan Pits Farm. Keep to the right of the ruins following the lane to a very awkward stile. Once over it a good grassy path leads you past a post which waymarks the Rossendale Way and takes you on to a second post close to a wall with a gap in it. (The shorter walk comes direct to this point.) Turn right through the gap and follow the path through the quarry, a collection of small excavations. Bear left at the first junction and right at the second. Soon after you will come to another post and then you strike fairly steeply down the hill following a good path. Keep going until you are opposite the reservoir embankment when you will see the tree and stile that lead you down to it and back to your car in a few minutes.

The Shorter Finish

From Causeway End bear left downhill towards the ruined farm visible about ½ mile away, there's no path but no problem. Continue in the same direction at this ruin. A faint path that becomes a ridge in the ground contours the hillside passing another ruined farm and leads to the gap in the wall by the post mentioned above. The post can be seen from quite a distance away.

Things of Interest

The three reservoirs in this valley were built at different dates as the need for water increased in the local towns. The first to be built was Calf Hey between 1854 and 1859, then came Holden Wood in 1897 but Ogden was not started until 1903 and finished in 1912.

Hog Low Pike is a mound of special interest because it just might be a burial mound like Round Loaf, Anglezarke. Evidence for this lies in its shape, its position on the edge of the moor, and its name, for Lowe is derived from an Anglo-Saxon word meaning burial place.

If you do this walk in winter on a fine day and find yourself at the wall corner above the Musbury Valley at about 2.00 p.m., look across the slopes to the right of the Tor. If conditions are right, you will see in three places a pattern of stripes running straight down the hill made by the sun casting shadows of sets of faint parallel ridges of earth not otherwise visible. They are probably the remains of some ancient field system.

Chimneys in quarries are most unusual, but Musbury Height Quarry seems to have been unusual in more ways than that. There is a vast area covered in spoil heaps, now well grown over, but nowhere is there any commensurate quarry face, only a collection of insignificant holes in the ground. The reason is that much of the quarrying was done underground. However, the chimney is the boldest remaining part of the engine house that evidently powered the haulage of waggons both on the ramp and down at least one incline. If you examine the path as it leaves the chimney you will see the remains of wooden railway sleepers still embedded in it. Further along, through the gate, you can see great paving stones with deep grooves that could only have been worn in them by the passage of the waggons. This path must then have been part of the incline system of the quarry.

Musbury Tor, Bull Hill and Musbury Heights from the Grane Valley

A WALK AROUND THE GRANE VALLEY   WALK NO. **3.10**

This walk goes right round the Grane Valley initially at a moderately high level but with little effort. It has exceptionally good and changing views even after 10 minutes and throughout its length. Worth saving for a good day! Its logical starting place is the Holden Arms Hotel at the junction of Haslingden road B6362 and Holcombe road, B6235, but unfortunately this means roadside parking in Holcombe road. It is easy to join the walk from the Clough Head car park which is only one field's length away.

    Time: about 4 hours. Light boots recommended.

From the Holden Arms to Deep Clough
Cross the road at the Holden Arms, walk past the cemetery and turn right at the end of it. Keep straight on at Holden Hall Farm and turn right at the end of the wall. Turn left in front of the barn ahead and follow a sunken track through a gate onto the open hillside. At this point spare a moment to look at the rearward view. Below is the spire of St. Stephen's church, beyond it that of Helmshore church. To its right is the flat top of Musbury Tor. To your left the reservoirs of the

143

Grane Valley are coming into view, but you will have to wait a little longer to see Pike Lowe above the nearer skyline. Keep to the lower track and follow the wall to a stile, go straight ahead through the wood and beyond it you will meet a farm access road. Follow this quite steeply up the hill to Cloud Farm. Keep straight on at the farm following the fence to a gate with a concealed stile on the right. Again keep straight on to the wall ahead where you will meet a well-marked cart track deeply grooved with tractor marks. This is the Rossendale Way. Follow this cart track for a good half mile. It contours the hillside at the foot of the escarpment staying at the top side of a wall, often broken down. You will have noticed two isolated trees ahead, when you have crossed the stile close to them you will meet a stony cart track. Turn left on it and follow it down the hill to a group of three trees close to a ruined farm. Now follows a tricky bit of trackless going across the rough pastures. Pass between the trees and the ruins, turn right at the end of the wall and continue to the next cross wall, only 100 yards or so. Turn left here and follow the line of the wall across the fields aiming at a solitary tree a little distance ahead. This tree is on the edge of the well named Deep Clough and below on the left is Heap Clough Quarry, still worked.

Deep Clough to Grane Road

Cross the clough to the tree on the other side and on the top side of the ruin there you will find the start of a path that becomes well-marked and walled in some places. It links a number of the former farms, now all in ruins, on this side of the valley. Follow it easily, climbing gently for about a mile. You will soon notice that you are above Clough Head car park. Frcm here you get a fine view of the upper part of the Grane Valley with Winter Hill, easily identified by its masts, beyond. You will cross a wire fence and stone stile immediately after, then the path stays on the top side of a substantial wall. Continue past a conifer plantation and in about 100 yards you will find a stile on the left. Cross this and cut down to the Grane road, keeping to the right a little to find the stile on to the road.

Grane Road to the Calf Hey Trail

Cross the road - take care, traffic is fast - turn left and go over the first stile just down the road. There is no path at first but bear diagonally right and you will come to a sunken cart track in about 100 yards. Turn right on it and follow it towards some quarry spoil heaps. Here it swings left and rapidly becomes a rush-filled groove, just follow its course gently down the hill where you will cross a tiny stream, no

Calf Hey Reservoir

more than a wet place in summer. Spare a few moments as you walk along to enjoy the truly excellent view of the reservoirs flanked by Cribden on the left and Musbury Heights on the right. The track is now walled and continues up the hill. Turn left through a gap in the wall 30 or 40 yards up the hill and contour the hillside above the ruined farm which you can see below you passing through a great bank of moss and rushes. Then drop down a little to reach a good walled track at the next ruin. Follow this track to some quite substantial ruins on the edge of a hollow which you cross by a narrow track. Climb up to the wall, cross the stile and turn right to reach the corner of the plantation. Keep going straight ahead passing a pair of isolated gate posts and keeping below a tiny quarry. Soon you pick up a well-trodden grassy track that runs down the hillside to a RW marker on a stone gate post. Now go slightly to the left to find another one and then aim for yet another pair of gate posts which are on the edge of the Calf Hey Trail at post 5.

The Calf Hey Trail to the Holden Arms

Turn right on the Trail and follow it to post 8. Here cross the little stream and as soon as you are up the steep bank, turn right. In about 60 or 70 yards look out for a solitary sycamore tree in the edge of the conifers on your left. Cut across to it and you will find a good path

145

The Ramp, Musbury Heights Quarry

through the wood leading you to two stiles. Cross them both and follow a narrow path on the bank of a ditch. It soon becomes a good path, easy to follow, and you have good views of the opposite side of the valley. Follow this track right past the end of the Ogden Reservoir.

At a junction of paths the Rossendale Way - which you have been following all this time - climbs up the hill, but you take the lower track. Follow this path right round the curve of the spoil heaps. You will come to the great incline down which stone from the Musbury Heights Quarry was lowered to a branch of the Accrington - Stubbins railway. There is a tunnel through it but prudence suggests that you go over it. Continue along the path taking the well signed diversion around a hay field at Rake Foot Farm, (called Tenements on the O.S. map). When you have crossed the stile immediately below the ruins of Old Rake Foot turn sharp left down the field to join the access road to Rake Foot Farm. Turn right on it and follow it back to the dam of Holden Wood Reservoir to the Holden Arms and your car.

The Route from Clough Head Quarry

A finger post in the middle of the picnic area points the way. The gravelled cart track leads you to a gate where you turn right to a pair of stiles. After the second one go straight up the field to join the route at the wall above.

Things of Interest

One of the most striking things about this walk is the number of ruined farms that is passes. Many of them were built during the first part of the eighteenth century when the growing population of the Lancashire towns required more land to be brought into cultivation in order to grow the food that was needed. At that time agricultural methods had seen little improvement since medieval times and this was the only way to increase food production. Marginal land, the fringes of the moors, was enclosed and farmhouses built in many places in upland Lancashire. Old Rake Foot Farm has a door lintel with the date 1718 and in its shippon the old stone flag partitions making stalls for a dozen cows can still be seen. By the early years of the nineteenth century British farming was suffering from a deep depression. Many of these hill farms which had used handloom weaving to eke out a living could no longer 'make a do' and fell into disuse and decay from that time.

For more background information about the reservoirs and the area in general, see the notes to the Calf Hey Trail.

4. WALKS AROUND DARWEN AND TOCKHOLES

More paths have been lost and stiles closed in the pastures to the east and south of Darwen than possibly anywhere else in the Area. Even the paths up Greystone Hill are lost in moorland growth and give walking that is too hard to be worthwhile, in fact a large chunk of land yields no worthwhile walking.

WALKING ON THE DARWEN MOORS   WALK NO.4.1

Being centrally placed within the West Pennine Moors Area, and having a network of good paths, these moors offer the very epitome of moorland walking - wide horizons, open skies, good going underfoot. Four short walks are given, but you can easily link Nos. 1 and 2 together for a longer one. Suitable for shoes in good dry conditions.

1.   Around the Northern End

Time: 1¼-1½ hours.

Start at The Royal Arms Hotel, Tockholes. This is on the minor road that leaves the A6062 at Ewood, Blackburn, and runs through Tockholes to join the A675 half-way between Belmont and Abbey Village. Park within the bus turning circle, there's room for a couple of dozen cars. There are also buses from Darwen and Blackburn.

Go through a gate at the right-hand side of a row of stone cottages called Hollinshead Terrace. A wide gravel track crosses the fields and then enters a wooded valley. A little way up this it makes a sharp horseshoe bend to the left. About 150 yards beyond the bend a green track cuts back on the right, at first easily, then steeply up to the remains of a seat. If you prefer, cut directly up to this track from the bend. It is obvious and very steep. At the seat turn left and follow the track that runs round the top edge of the moor to the Tower. Climb the staircase within the Tower and enjoy the shelter of the 'greenhouse' on the top if it's windy. There's a grand view from it.

149

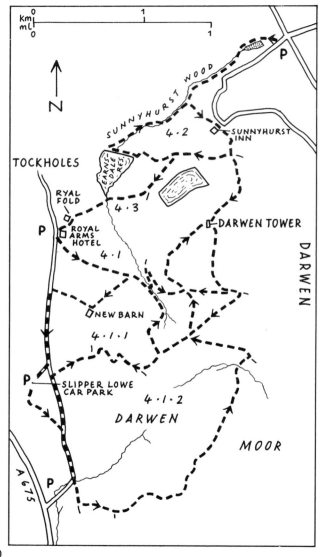

Darwen Tower

Three stainless steel plates have been let into the stonework on the top of the balcony. They purport to indicate the names of the various hills around in some detail but are extremely confusing if not in error. (See Walk No.4.2 for a note of what you really can see.) The track now runs round the edge of the moor overlooking Darwen. Follow it round and across a wide hollow and take the second path to the right. This one runs back over the highest point of the moor to Lyon's Den, a ruined farmhouse at the head of the little valley where you started. The path that you are following is joined by others that criss-cross the moor, but keep aiming at the head of the valley where the path curves gently into it. Now follow the track down the valley to the horseshoe bend where you will re-join the path where you started.

Another starting point, giving a longer walk, is the Sunnyhurst Inn Darwen. See Walk No.4.12 for details on how to find it and get to

Darwen Tower from it. Then follow the above walk until you meet a good path coming in on your right at a sharp angle. Turn right on it and almost at once you will find another one going off left that runs around the edge of the moor and will bring you back to the Tower.

Time for this walk: about 2 hours.

2. The Central Part

Time: 1¼-1½ hours.

Park at the end of the minor road mentioned above just before it joins the A675. There is plenty of room. Alternatively park at Slipper Lowe car park. To find it continue from the Royal Hotel for about a mile then turn right down a lane in the trees. Set off from the car park as for Walk No.4.8, 'A Visit to the Wishing Well of Hollinshead Hall'. As you approach the Well keep straight on through an open gateway. The stone chipping path will take you to a stile onto the road where you turn right. If you use this start turn right not left on the road when you return to find the car park.

Walk along this road to its first sharp corner. There you will find a stile leading to a grass track. After about 200 yards take the left-hand branch. It climbs gently past a ruined farm to a wall on the top of the moor. Don't go astray on a left-hand branch. At the top by the wall is an old seat with a fine view and a finger post indicating the way to Belmont, Darwen and Turton. Take the path to Darwen at the second cairn. It passes two old mineworkings and crosses over to the Darwen side of the moor. As it starts to drop down and swing to the right, you will see another track coming up from Darwen, one that goes back over the moor to Lyon's Den. Take this track, keep left at the next junction, and keep on until you reach Lyon's Den. Here, instead of turning down the valley, take the track that crosses an old bridge and then climb up to the skyline. Go through the fence and drop down to the road by the wide grass track. Turn left on the road and 15 minutes of gentle downhill walking will return you to your car.

3. The Combined Walk

Time: about 2½ hours.

If you want to make a real afternoon of it over these moors, start and finish by the second of the two walks described above. When you have passed the old pits and have reached the track coming up from Darwen, turn right on it and drop down a little into the valley until you can see a small track by a wall on the left climbing up on to the edge of the moor again. Follow this until you come to the Tower. This bit of track gives fine views over Darwen including a 'close-up' view of the elaborate chimney at India Mill. From the Tower follow the track along the northern and western edges of the moor. Where the path forks above the little valley, take the left-hand branch following a fence. Cross the next path that comes in from the left and continue slightly rightward. The path then goes through the fence and down slightly to Lyon's Den at the head of the little valley. there you re-join the second route. Definitely the best walk on the Darwen Moors.

4. Darwen Tower from Slippery Lowe Car Park

The Tower is not as easily reached from this car park as from the Royal Hotel, Tockholes, (Walk No.4.1.1). It uses some of the same tracks that characterize the walking on Darwen Moor and is in no way inferior.

Time: allow a little longer, towards 2 hours.

Return to the tarmac road from the car park and turn right. About 100 yards away you will see a finger post to Lyon's Den, a ruined house on the moor. Folow the good wide track over the brow of the hill and down the other side, cross two small streams and continue, climbing gently all the time, to a gate and stile. It will probably take you around 30 minutes from your car.

Go through the gate and take the left-hand track at the Y-junction that faces you. After about 50 yards take another left-hand track that goes across the moor to join another one close to the remains of an old seat and a stile. Keep straight on here and pick up the main track that runs around the northern edge of Darwen Moor to the Tower. Don't be tempted to make a bee-line for the Tower, even though you seem to be walking away from it, there's some rough going in between. See Walk No.4.2 for details of the view from the Tower.

Leave the Tower by the same path used by Walk No.4.1.1, the one that curves round a great hollow in the moor, but on this walk you turn right at the **first** path to leave on the right. It cuts back at quite an acute angle but takes you across the moor to the stile above. Now cross the stile and keep straight on down the wide grassy track to the cart track that runs in a horseshoe around the head of Stepback Brook below you - or take the steep direct descent if you prefer.

Turn left on the cart track and when you reach the gate at the end of the wood turn left in front of it and follow the track by the wall to New Barn Farm. Turn right between the buildings and carry on to the road. Turn left and 5 or 6 minutes will see you back to your car.

Things of Interest

Most people associate freedom of access to the moors with Derbyshire:

153

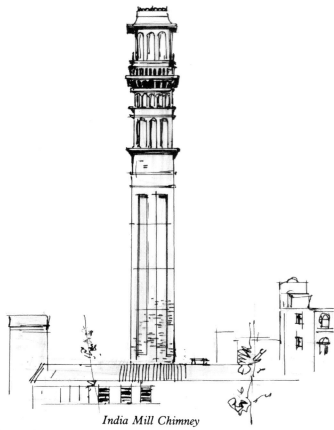

India Mill Chimney

few know that they owe their freedom to walk the Darwen Moors to the public spirited action of a few Darwen men led by Mr. W.T.Ashton. The struggle began in 1878, when many of the rights of way established during the heyday of the coal mining industry on the moors were becoming blocked and paths destroyed by the owners of the sporting rights. Mr. Ashton, who had a good knowledge of the rights of way, organised what became a long drawn out legal battle, and on his death in 1894, his sons purchased the shooting rights of Darwen Moor Common and vested them in the Corporation. On the

154

death of the Lord of the Manor free access to the rest of the moor was also vested in the Corporation. On Sept. 6th 1896 a large procession went over the moor to the spot where the Tower now stands to celebrate the freedom of the moors. (See Walk No.4.2 for a note about the Tower.)

As just noted many of the good tracks that cross the moor were made for access to the old coal pits whose spoil heaps are dotted around. The shafts of these pits were originally lined with stone, but most of them have crumbled and weathered to a cone shaped hollow. Some are full of water, others of earth. The first one that you pass on the second walk (above) has its stone lining in good condition and is worth a cautious look. The lining seems to reach down for 25 or 30 feet, until it reaches good solid rock. If you toss a stone down, it goes a long way in several bounces before it stops. These old shafts were about 200ft. deep - quite shallow by modern mining standards. They worked the Upper Mountain Seam, which varied from 24 to 42 inches thick. The Lower Mountain Seam outcrops in Stepback Brook where the first walk starts and was once mined there.

Hollinshead Terrace at Tockholes was built as a row of mill cottages by Eccles Shorrock, a Darwen cotton manufacturer, for the workers at his nearby factory, now demolished and vanished. The same man also built India Mill whose campanile-like chimney can be seen so well from the moors. It was built in 1867, is 300ft. high, and its huge foundation stone was quarried at Cadshaw. (See Walk No.2.2.)

SUNNYHURST WOODS AND DARWEN TOWER
WALK NO.4.2

Where else in the Area is there a walk leading to the moors that starts within 100 yards of the main road in the centre of a town and goes right to the top only crossing a tarmac road once?

Time: 1 hour, 1 hour 40 minutes return.

Approaching from Blackburn along the A666, about a mile after crossing the borough boundary, you will see the Co-operative Stores on the right. The main entrance to the woods is at the end of Falcon Avenue, which is the street on its right, but it is better to turn right into Earnsdale Street which is next to St. Cuthbert's Church. Park behind the church and cut through a side street to Falcon Avenue: the entrance to the woods is just 50 yards away.

Walk up the main pathway into the wooded valley, past the Visitor Centre and café, then take the first left-hand branch of the path, near

155

a curious roofed structure, possibly at one time a bandstand. The path climbs steeply upwards and comes out on the road through a pleasing lichgate, Potter's Gate. Turn left, and opposite the Sunnyhurst Inn, 50 yards further on, a rough lane goes off to the right. Follow this past an old quarry, through a gate up onto the moor. Where the track branches, take the right-hand one. Almost immediately you can see the Tower, and you will reach it in another 5 minutes. The views to the north and east are the best in the whole Area. You can almost always see the great hump of Pendle and the long ridge of Longridge Fell close at hand, with the Bowlands behind Longridge. Often you will see Blackpool Tower and Black Combe, the most westerly of the Lakeland Hills. More rarely, if you look up the Ribble Valley you can see Ingleborough with Whernside on its immediate left. Penyghent is much further to the right and is not so easily picked out. You can see Holcombe Hill with Peel's Monument to the south-east, but views in that direction are not particularly good.

Instead of returning by the same route, you can extend the walk by returning the full length of Sunnyhurst Woods. Allow an extra 20-30 minutes. Return as far as the old quarry, then turn left through a gateway into a narrow walled lane that crosses the field to a new concrete road. Turn right on this, then left where it joins a rough road 50 yards further on. Turn right immediately after the house onto a cart track. This track goes to the dam on the Earnsdale Reservoir. Follow it to the last iron gate, where on the right you will see a stile leading to the top end of Sunnyhurst Woods. Follow whichever selection of paths you like. All downhill paths lead to the road.

If, on the other hand, you haven't much time for a visit to the Tower drive up the road by the church. At the top of the hill the road swings left and the Sunnyhurst Inn is on the right. It is possible to park at the roadside, and you can pick up the route just described at that point.

Things of Interest

Sunnyhurst Woods are really a Corporation park, with the usual network of neat paths and bridges over the stream. Prior to 1800 the area was farm land, then some tree planting was done to give cover for game birds. The woods were acquired by Darwen Corporation in 1902 to celebrate the coronation of King Edward VII. In common with most town woodlands in this district, they are mainly sycamore, beech, oak, hawthorn and rhododendron. Marsh marigolds and bluebells abound in the spring, and in one place there is a colony of golden saxifrage, an inconspicuous and relatively rare plant. In fact the Area is rich in plant and bird life, as many as 96 species of plants have been found. Higher up the woods bilberry and heather grow in patches, and these plants, together with mat grass, dominate the moorland vegetation.

The old keeper's cottage is now a Visitor Centre with changing displays of the natural history of the Area. It also houses a fascinating collection of old photographs showing the woods as they used to be. The Centre is open on Tuesdays, Thursdays, Saturdays and Sundays, 2.00-4.30 p.m. Admission is free. Outside the house is an old fashioned cottage garden where every plant is named - pure delight for the gardener. For those with a deeper botanical interest there is a collection of named ferns in the yard at the side. Ferns, like grasses, are very tricky to identify, and this collection is a great help.

Close by is the Old England Café where light refreshments are available. It was erected in 1911-12 by public subscription to commemorate the coronation of King George V.

The Tower itself was built in 1897 by the Corporation to mark Queen Victoria's Diamond Jubilee. They seemed rather good at those things then. As so often happens the Tower was later neglected and fell into disrepair. It was restored by public subscription in 1972.

FROM DARWEN TO RYAL FOLD, TOCKHOLES
WALK NO.4.3

This walk describes a circular tour starting at Sunnyhurst Woods and returning by the local Darwen Tower. Alternatively you can return on the bus to either Darwen or Blackburn.

Time: about 2 hours, possibly more depending on the variation you take.

Start the walk through Sunnyhurst Woods exactly as described in Walk No.4.2. When you come to the bandstand keep straight on instead of bearing left at that point. After that, keep right whenever there is a choice of path - there's plenty and it doesn't matter much which you take as they all come out at the Earnsdale Reservoir dam. Cross the dam if you've come out at the right-hand side and follow the cart track until if joins another at a sharp angle. Turn right here and leave this second cart track after a short ½ mile by a pleasant footpath that drops down to the reservoir level and then climbs steadily up through the fields by a clear path and line of stiles to Ryal Fold. Then straight ahead along the lane you will find the road, the Royal Arms Hotel, and the bus stop.

Here you are at the start of the Roddlesworth Nature Trail (Walk No.4.6) and of the walk that goes round the northern end of Darwen Moor. It is well worthwhile doing the first part of this walk as far as the Tower on your return, for the views are excellent. Then return to your car by going down the wide path on your left as you face Darwen. At the tarmac turn left and just beyond the Sunnyhurst Inn you will find the lych gate into the woods.

Alternatively, instead of making the fairly steep ascent from Stepback Brook, keep on this track through Higher Wenshead and you will find you are on the track you used after climbing up from Earnsdale Reservoir. Instead of retracing your steps keep straight on this track. It will bring you to the lych gate into Sunnyhurst Woods and you can return this way.

Things of Interest

See Walk No.4.2 for the notes on Sunnyhurst Woods and Walk No.4.4 for the notes about Tockholes. Ryal Fold is a group of old farmhouses, one of which has been very pleasantly restored. If you do the walk in late June before the hay has been cut, you will see they don't grow grass round Tockholes, just flowers!

A LOOK AROUND TOCKHOLES   WALK NO.4.4

Tockholes, pronounced 'Tockles' for the benefit of the uninitiated, isn't just a village like Belmont or Turton, nor is it a suburb of Blackburn. It's a rural area of considerable charm nestling on the western slopes of Winter Hill, not *the* Winter Hill, but another one in the north-west corner of the Area. It isn't even on a road to anywhere in particular, and some of the most interesting buildings lie on a loop road below the minor road on which the biggest cluster of houses and shops stand.

To find this charming corner by road, get onto the minor road that runs from the Brown Cow on Livesey Branch Road, Ewood, Blackburn, to the Preston-Belmont road (A675). From Blackburn continue up the hill until you reach the Rock Inn. There is no public car park in Tockholes at present and you have to be cheeky and use either the car park at the Rock Inn, or that at the Village Hall a little further on, or that of the Victoria Hotel a little further on still.

It's best to park at any one of these and then explore the loop road on foot as this is extremely narrow, and parking, except by St. Stephen's Church, is almost impossible. Besides, it's a lovely walk

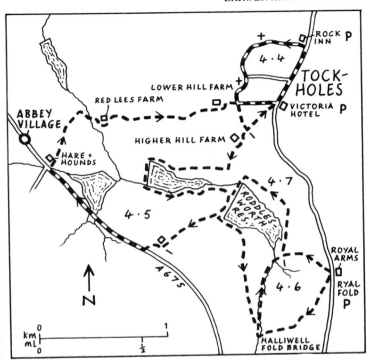

along lanes heavy with the scent of hawthorn, elder flower and haymaking on a good summer's day. Allow an hour for it. There are buses from Darwen and Blackburn. Wherever you are parked go to the Rock Inn.

The Rock Inn itself, though of modern appearance, has a datestone for the year 1791. Turn down the lane besides the Inn and continue steeply down the hill to the vicarage and church. The vicarage wall has built into it an old stone archway dated 1692, and a little lower down a double Norman arch spans a well, built into the wall. A worn, almost illegible inscription at the back tells you that this archway was brought from Garstang Hall when it was demolished in 1903 and re-erected by the vicar of that time. Unfortunately the pipe that feeds the well no longer runs. Pass on, entering the churchyard by the lych gate. On the

159

Tockholes School

right you will see Tockholes' first school built in 1854, and now being restored.

Its most interesting feature is an external pulpit. You can imagine the crowds seated on the grass beneath the trees when congregations were bigger than today. Go on to the Church of St. Stephen, a very pleasing modern structure incorporating a fragment from an earlier building. There has been a series of churches on this site dating from 884 A.D. Of similar antiquity is the Toches Stone which stands on the left just before you reach the church. The base on which the stone stands bears the following explanatory inscription:

'The upper portion of this monument is supposed to be a remnant of the old parish preaching cross, probably dating to 884 A.D. The lower portion is probably a part of the ancient Toches Stones from which the parish takes it name.'

There is an interesting reminder of the Industrial Revolution in this churchyard - John Balderston's grave. It lies behind the church on the right and states simply:

John Balderston
Inventor of the weft fork
Born 1780   Died 1862

Like many inventors, Balderston made no money out of his invention and died a pauper. Though not of such outstanding importance as

160

Lower Hill Farm, Tockholes

Crompton's spinning mule, cotton manufacturers of the time made plenty of money out of it, and erected this memorial some time after his death.

Now leave the churchyard and continue along the lane. In a few hundred yards you will come to another church, Tockholes United Reformed Church, founded in 1662, re-built in 1710 and again in 1880. Non-conformism has always been strong in the moorland villages, nowhere more than here. On Black Bartholomew's Day 1662, the people of Tockholes refused to adopt the Prayer Book under the Act of Uniformity and left the Church to establish their own form of worship. So too, did the people of Rivington.

Continue a little further along the lane and there, on the right is the site of another church, the Bethesda Mortuary Chapel, fittingly with its own graveyard. No wonder the whole district is known as Chapels! Spare a glance for the row of cottages on your left, if you have time, turn right for a diversion to Lower Hill Farm, a fine old house and a Grade 2 listed building. Then keep straight on up the footpath. It's an ordinary footpath between wide walls, but most curiously, has a pair of regulation Ministry of Transport signs saying, 'No road for motor vehicles except for access'. They'd have a job! The footpath turns

161

sharp left behind the row of cottages on your left at the top of the hill, and takes you back to the centre of the village opposite the Victoria, but before doing that, continue further up the lane as far as Rose Cottage (the junction with Walk No.4.5) and look to your right to see Higher Hill Farm. It's another fine old farmhouse whose main claim to fame is its 'lofty loo', still to be seen jutting out into fresh air on the first floor of the east wall. It must have been a great convenience in the days of primitive sanitation.

Back to the Victoria, then, a mock Tudor affair with black wooden beams bolted onto a solid stone building just for effect. Still, it's not unpleasing. Here you are back to the road on which the Rock Inn stands. Turn left, and less than 10 minutes will see you there.

TOCKHOLES AND THE LOWER RODDLESWORTH
RESERVOIR   WALK NO.4.5

This is a splendid circular walk that passes three of the most picturesque old farms in the Area, and takes you through flower-filled fields and woodland. It can be combined with the previous walk.

Time: 1¼ hour or 2 hours if you combine with Walk No.4.4.

See the previous walk for instructions for finding Tockholes and parking. Wherever you park make your way to the Victoria Hotel. Across the road in the corner of School Lane there is a stile. Follow the path by the wall all the way to Higher Hill where it emerges from the fields below an old quarry. Continue about 100 yards to Rose Cottage.

Turn right immediately you have passed Rose Cottage, and about 50 yards down the lane turn left into a pasture. The stile has a whitewashed reminder, 'Keep your dog on a lead'. First, however, go ahead a little in order to have a better look at Higher Hill Farm, yet another of these fine old farms. Back to the stile. The path is faint, but follow the wall on the right to its end then turn right and go straight down the hill to a white gate that leads you into the woods. Follow the woodland path to the forestry road. Turn right on it and follow it along the fringe of the wood to the dam of the Lower Roddlesworth Reservoir. Cross the dam and the graceful new wooden footbridge beyond it. Turn left and follow the delightful waterside path to the base of the dam of the upper reservoir. Cross the outfall by a stone slab bridge and follow a little path up the slope to the right to join the wide track - almost a road - into the woods. Follow this track to the farm, where, surprise, surprise, the gate across this track is locked. Saved again! There's a stile in the corner by the barn and the wall. This

Red Lees Farm, Tockholes

brings you into the farmyard from where a cart track leads to the main road. 10 minutes along it will see you at the Hare and Hounds in Abbey Village. See page 33 for some notes about this unusual mill village.

Turn right onto a cart track by the side of the pub. Follow this through the riding school and down into the wooded valley then to Red Lees Farm. Alternatively you can go across the wooded footbridge when you will climb very steeply into the farmyard.

Red Lees Farm is one of the oldest in the Area with a datestone of 1674 and has been carefully restored. If you have come up the farm road turn right into a lane as soon as you are through the farm gate, but you'll miss the front of the house unless you pop round to the left. If you come by the footbridge, you will be facing it.

Follow this grassy lane (muddy in wet weather), and when you have passed the first bend, look up to the fence on the left to spot the stile by the gate; it's easier to see from here. Only cross over to it when you're at the end of the lane, as the field is often cultivated hay. The path through the pasture is faint, but the stile at the end is into a

163

grassy lane. This takes you past Lower Hill, in some ways even more attractive than Red Lees, and onto a bit of tarmac road at Victoria Terrace. Follow it up the hill to the main road.

Things of Interest
See Walk No.4.5 for notes about Tockholes. If you turn left where you join the road at Victoria Terrace you can wander along to have a look at St. Stephen's Church. Add about 30 minutes to the time if you do this. The two Roddlesworth reservoirs and the Lower Rake Brook Reservoir were built by Liverpool Corporation at about the same time as the Anglezarke and Rivington reservoirs. Water from the Roddlesworth Reservoir flows into the Anglezarke Reservoir through the Goit, best seen at White Coppice. (See Walk No.1.10).

THE RODDLESWORTH NATURE TRAIL, TOCKHOLES
WALK NO.4.6

This walk starts almost opposite the Royal Arms Hotel, Tockholes. A pamphlet describing it is available at the various Visitor Centres. It will take you about an hour just to do the walk, more if you start hunting for and identifying plants. Whether or not this is your particular interest, this walk is quite the finest and longest woodland and stream-side walk in the whole Area. The walk has been extended since the first edition of this book and now goes to the bank of the Upper Roddlesworth Reservoir where there is a marvellous surprise view.

To find the Royal Arms Hotel, get onto the minor road that runs from Ewood, Blackburn to join the A675 Preston-Bolton road near Belmont. From Blackburn the road climbs steadily and you pass three more pubs, until, almost below Darwen Tower, you will find the Royal Arms. Park within the bus turning circle. There is room for a couple of dozen cars. If the day is good a superb view, almost as good as that from Darwen Tower, and without effort. The route is marked with red topped posts, unfortunately missing here and there but it is easy to follow except where noted in this text. Any variations within it are quite minor and lead to the same place.

The Nature Trail Committee has done a great deal of work to improve the path with gravel and steps and it is suitable for shoes and any weather. It is worth noting that the return from the river is long and steep - elderly people will find it easier to do the walk the other way round. There is a map at the start and you need little guidance to follow the way. Take care to follow the riverside path at the bridge and when you reach the reservoir bank, with its marvellous surprise view, turn right up the hill **before** you cross the little stream. There is no marker at present, (Autumn 1986.)

Things of Interest
The Roddlesworth Nature Trail was sponsored by the Tockholes Women's Institute during European Conservation Year, 1970. Local residents designed and manage the trail and are assisted by North West Conservation volunteers and local scouts. The present Trail Guide describes the route and what is to be seen at the various stations and is extremely well done. There is probably a greater variety of interesting subjects than on any other nature trail within the Area.

THE RODDLESWORTH RESERVOIRS   WALK NO.4.7

The North West Water Authority have recently opened a number of their paths round the two Roddlesworth reservoirs to the public. Their action has made available a quiet and secluded area which gives good opportunites for bird watching. Particular care should be taken to avoid polluting the water or causing fires. It is best visited from the car park at Ryal Fold, Tockholes. See Walk No.4.4 for instructions. Allow 1 hour or a little more for the shorter version, 1¾ hours for the longer one. Both will be suitable for shoes and all weathers when the NWWA have carried out their planned path improvement work.

Start by the return path of the Nature Trail, in other words by the right-hand path when you stand with your back to the car park. Follow this path until you meet a forestry road. (Actually its end in 1986 but it will be continued to Halliwell Fold Bridge during 1987.) Turn right on this road and follow it through the woods where there are glimpses of the water through the trees. The road climbs easily almost to the top of the woods, where a branch (see alternative below) makes a sharp curve left down to the iron bridge over the spillway and then crosses the dam.

Turn left at the end of the dam and follow the path to the stile that gives access to the reservoir shore for anglers. Here you bear right along a path through mature woodland, with stately oak, ash and beech trees, a delight in autumn when their leaves carpet the woodland floor. This path will take you to Halliwell Fold Bridge where you join the Nature Trail. If you cross the bridge and turn left you take the shortest route back to Ryal Fold, but if you turn left following the stream you will go down to the reservoir again and can return by your starting path. Well worth doing for the sake of the surprise view if you have a little time in hand.

Alternatively you can keep straight on and continue to the lower dam. See the previous walk for details, but bear left instead of right when you approach the upper dam and join this walk there.

Things of Interest
These reservoirs were built by Liverpool Corporation in 1855 as part of their Rivington Scheme. They collect water from the north-eastern end of the moorland and it is transferred to the Anglezarke Reservoir through the Goit. They are used by fly fishermen so take care to keep well away from the water's edge lest you catch the backlash of one of their casts. Wild duck may be seen in late autumn and winter -mallard and golden eye are common, occasionally tufted duck, great crested grebes and Canada geese. All can be observed from the screen of the woodland's edge.

A VISIT TO THE WISHING WELL OF HOLLINSHEAD HALL
WALK NO.4.8

The Well lies east of the Bolton-Preston road A675, two miles south of Abbey Village but is not marked on the map.

The Well is best visited from the Slipper Lowe car park, Tockholes Road. To find this, see Walk No.4.4. Allow 30-40 minutes for the

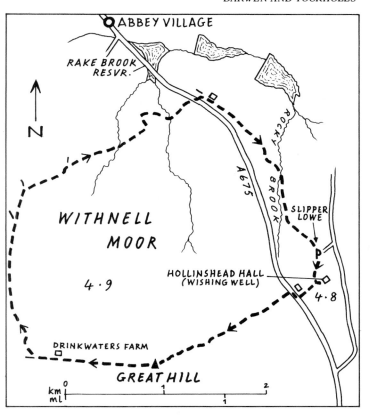

Map showing route around Withnell Moor, with Abbey Village, Rake Brook Resvr., A675, Rocky Brook, Slipper Lowe, Hollinshead Hall (Wishing Well), Drinkwaters Farm, and Great Hill. Scale shown in km and ml.

return trip. Continue in the direction you entered the car park to the rough road beyond, turn left, bear left at the fork, and keep straight ahead until you meet a path coming in from the right. You can now see the Well House straight ahead a few minutes away. An alternative approach is by a footpath starting about 100 yards south of a farm called, strangely, Piccadilly. This is the first building on the east side of the road if you are travelling south from Abbey Village. You can just park on the verge, but you need to be careful, it is a fast road.

Time: 30-40 minutes for the return trip.

Go through the swing gate and follow the path through the trees for about 10 minutes. You will soon be able to see the Well House as a small barn-like building on the right.

Go into the Well House. It's a bit dark, but you will soon see water pouring from the mouth of a stone lion into a deep trough and then into two deep recesses on either side of the lion. It is quite impressive and a little bit eerie.

The date of the building is not known, though the style may be described as rural Georgian. It may have been built when the nearby Hollinshead Hall, now utterly ruined and vanished, was re-built in 1776. The building was restored by Liverpool Corporation in 1905. The Well was known in medieval times and reputed to have curative properties for eye troubles. In fact, the water is diverted from a tiny stream nearby into a sort of tank behind the building and then to the lion. The Well House is now a listed building.

You may also visit the Wishing Well by making a long extension to the Roddlesworth Nature Trail from Halliwell Fold Bridge, but as it involves a long uphill trudge on a rough wet lane it is not recommended. There are plans to restore the foundations of Hollinshead Hall and to make a trail similar to the one at Grane.

GREAT HILL, WITHNELL MOOR AND ROCKY BROOK
WALK NO.4.9

An excellent walk with good views from Withnell Moor. Here the paths are untrodden but a field by field description of the tricky bit is given.

Time: allow 3-3½ hours, possibly more. Boots are strongly recommended.

Walk down the short lane from the Slipper Lowe car park to its junction with another old rough lane. Turn left here and keep left at the fork a few yards ahead. Turn right at the T-junction and follow the stony path to the road, the A675. Cross it with care for it is a fast road, turn right and left almost at once over the stile. The well-trodden and often very wet path leads quite quickly to the top of Great Hill. There are a number of minor variants that try - in vain - to avoid the wet, but there are no problems in crossing the stream. Great Hill has good views over the coast and to the north and west.

From the cairn continue in the direction you have been taking passing the ruins of Drinkwaters Farm in its sheltering trees. A few minutes beyond the farm turn right at the path junction - it is signed for Brinscall. Follow this cart track, often very wet, until you meet the wall, then turn right and follow it along the wall until it brings you to a stile onto the lane that leads down to Brinscall. Go straight across this lane into another one that ends in about 400 yards by a ruined barn.

Now the tricky bit starts. The track you have been following now swings right into a green field, but you keep straight ahead aiming for the wall not far away. Turn right and follow it until you come to a pair of stone gate posts. Turn left here onto a good track which forks in about 50 yards. Take the right-hand one which will bring you to a gap in the wall - and then disappears. Keep on in the same direction aiming for a pair of grassy humps in the middle distance (Winter Hill above Tockholes). The going is quite rough for a short distance but when you top the heathery rise it improves. Here you should be able to see Rake Brook Reservoir below on your left. Now change your direction slightly aiming at Darwen Tower. Shortly you will drop down into a stream, unnamed on the map, and you should be close to the Stepping Stones marked on the map. They are no longer there. The key to further progress is in the new stile over the wire fence just above the place where it crosses the stream. Continue in the same direction and in a very few moments you will see a pair of wooden gate posts ahead. Make for them and then follow the wall close to them down to a cross wall. Here you will find yourself on a good cart track. Turn left and follow it for a few minutes until you come to a gate across it with a stile. Here turn right and follow the fence to the road, the A675. Note that the stream can be quite difficult to cross after heavy rain. The bridge has long since disappeared.

Go straight across the road to a stile into a short green lane that puts you onto a farm access road. Turn right on this and after passing two farms and a barn it will bring you to the bridge over Rocky Brook. Cross the bridge and turn right on the wide, rough, and often wet track that will lead you back to the short lane leading to the car park.

Views from Withnell Moor

At the start of the tricky section there are wide views of the Ribble Estuary, Blackpool Tower, even the Lake District's western edge if the day is clear. To the right of them is the long ridge of Longridge Fell with Kemple End marking its right-hand end. The Bowlands lie behind it, almost completely masked. As you turn more to the right Pendle Hill comes into view and finally Darwen Tower. Between them, rather distant, there are some of the lesser hills of the Yorkshire Dales.

The lane you return by was once the coach road to Hollinshead Hall. See Walk No.4.7 for more about it.

Stepback Brook, Darwen Moors

THE THREE TOWERS OF LANCASHIRE WALK NO.5.1

This is the great classic walk of the Area, taking in the towers of Rivington, Darwen, and Holcombe. It is usually done from Georges Lane, Horwich, to Holcombe and will take 7½-8½ hours. Many variations are possible, but the route described here does not look for difficulties and uses a fair number of paths not otherwise covered in this book. It is best to park in Bolton and to use public transport for the start and finish, though unfortunately this virtually rules out Sundays.

Take the bus from Moor Lane bus station, Bolton, to Georges Lane, Horwich, and follow that lane right to the Pike. 30-40 minutes is sufficient to see you there, a useful boost to morale! Return to the rough moorland road that Georges Lane has become and follow it to its junction with the Belmont-Rivington road. (A more sporting walk takes in Winter Hill. Passing the TV masts, turn left to the Post Office mast and keeping left until the O.S. cairn is seen on the right. Then drop down to the road, re-joining the main route.)

Just over the crest of the road you will see a gate on the left. A wettish track runs down towards Belmont from it. As you approach the wall on the right look out for a stile and continue to Belmont by a cinder track.

Turn left when you reach the main road. In about 2-3 hundred yards a short cut footpath leads down to the road that crosses the dam. As soon as you are across the dam take the farm road that leads to Lower and Higher Pasture Houses. As you go through the farm the track tends to the right a bit and then joins a cart track. Turn left on this and follow it until it reaches the road. Keep on this road for a good half mile until you see a broad grassy track on the right. It is signposted 'Footpath to Lyon's Den'. Follow this track up the side of Cartridge Hill and go through a stile in the wall on the top of the ridge.

You can now see Darwen Tower quite clearly, but it doesn't pay to make a bee-line for it. Keep to the track you are on, cross the old stone bridge and keep straight ahead, climbing just a little. After about 5 minutes there is a three-way junction of tracks. You want the left-hand one which runs parallel to the valley on your left, whilst dropping down slightly. Go straight ahead at the next 'crossroads', still bearing left a little, until you meet the track that climbs up the valley and contours the edge of the moor on the north side and leads to the Tower. This is Tower No.2 safely in the bag. Now comes the hard part! Turn south and follow the good track that runs round the edge of the moor overlooking Darwen until it drops down into a steep-sided

171

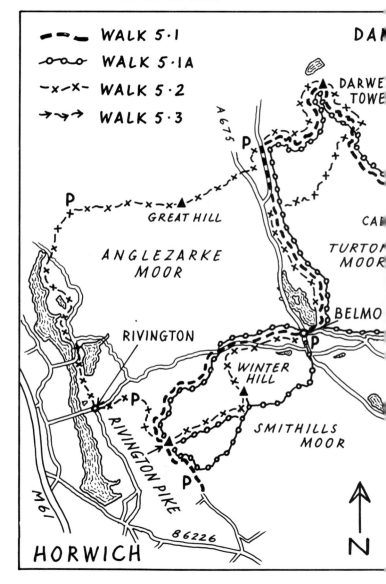

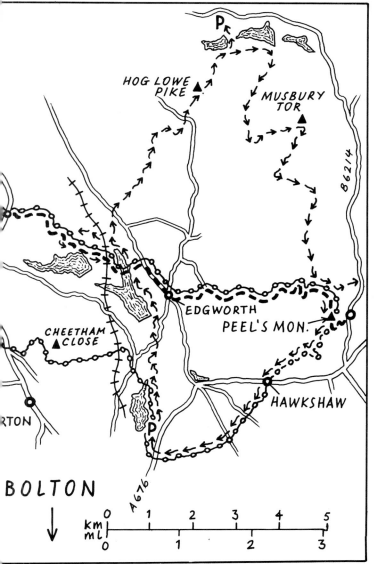

P

HOG LOWE
PIKE ▲

MUSBURY
TOR ▲

B6214

EDGWORTH
PEEL'S MON. ▲

CHEETHAM
▲ CLOSE

HAWKSHAW

RTON

P

BOLTON
↓

A676

km
ml

0   1   2   3   4   5

0   1   2   3

valley, Duckshaw Brook. Then turn right on the tarmac road that comes up this valley. Leave it for an ill define wet path where it swings right to the house above. Follow this wet path for ⅓ mile round the curve of the moor until it starts to go leftwards. Here you leave it, and it is most important to find the right place or you will have much trouble finding the way over to Cadshaw. There are three tracks, all faint, crossing the moor in various places, and yours is the last one. There is a row of three farms below you as you come along after crossing the brook. The last one has a newish tile roof. Go well past this until you meet a fence coming right down across the track you're on, except for a gap for walkers. Go through this gap, turn right, and follow the line of the fence.

The going is pretty rough, but it improves. Cross the next fence - there's no stile - and turn left at the next one. The fence becomes a wall. Follow this to a properly constructed sheep gap on the right. Through the gap bear left and follow a rushy hollow until you meet a cart track coming in from the left. These are hay fields, in summer, walk their boundaries. Follow this through several fields and at the gate keep straight on. Follow this well-marked track down to the road.

Turn left on the road and go up the hill for about 200 yards to where a wide cart track labelled 'Public Footpath' leaves on the right. It runs between walls right down to the Turton and Entwistle Reservoir. About a mile along it, take the right-hand fork. Shortly after arriving at the reservoir side, you leave it again by a narrow track that runs through the trees and over a field to join the lane that goes down to Entwistle station. Go past the station and across the dam and up to the Edgworth road, where you turn right.

In Edgworth go across the crossroads and turn left down a cart track by the side of the Rose and Crown, and follow it up to the tarmac road, the last bit met on this walk. Turn right and keep straight on along a track after the tarmac ends in a couple of hundred yards. This track will bring you to Redearth Farm and continues beyond it towards the moor. Roughly one field's length beyond the farm it swings left and there is a pair of field gates on the right. Behind them, not obvious at present, is a newly fenced-in path to Lower Grainings Farm. This is where you go. At its end make to the right of the barn ahead and onto the lane. (Work is still in progress and there may be further changes.)

Spare a moment to look at the tiny tree-fringed burial ground on your right as you come onto the lane. It contains just one tombstone, or rather two for the same grave: the original one now cracked and repaired and cracked yet again and a modern one by its side. This one tells just a little of the story. Roger Worthington was a Baptist minister who died in 1709 aged about 50. It is said that he came from a Roman Catholic family who disowned him when he rejected their faith. Whatever the truth he doesn't seem to have been attached to a church but to have been a hermit or a wandering preacher amongst the moorland folk who were strong Non-conformists.

Follow the lane to the T-junction, and there keep staight ahead to Holcombe Hey Fold. Go through the farm passing to the left of the last building and going through two gates in quick succession. Now follow the faint track that contours the base of the steep ground. Cut across to the ruins of Holcombe Head Farm and climb up the hill very steeply and without a track at first, aiming just to the right of Harcles Hill. You will find the track when you cross under the power lines, if not before. Then follow it across the moor and round to the monument. There! You've done it! Tower No.3 is in the bag.

All that remains is to get down to Holcombe Brook for public transport. Follow the sign to Holcombe Village. When you reach Moorbottom Road turn left and in a few yards turn right into Holcombe Old Road. Follow this for a good half mile to the main road at Holcombe Brook. The bus stop is opposite, with an hourly service, and the Hare and Hounds is on your right.

THE CIRCUIT OF THE THREE TOWERS   WALK NO.5.1A

You may prefer to try a circuit of the Towers rather than tolerate the delays of public transport. It is in the 30 mile plus class and will take around an extra 3 hours compared with the linear version.

It is better to start from Belmont rather that Georges Lane, Horwich. Ideally, use the Black Dog's car park, but fix it with the landlord first. Failing that, park at the Blue Lagoon on the Rivington road.

If you are parked at the 'Dog' walk down the main road for a few minutes. At the far end of the wood you will find a stile. Follow the wettish path up the hillside until it joins the wide track that runs from the Wright's Arms to the top of Winter Hill. Note that it crosses a farm access track on the way. Bear left when you reach the tarmac.

If you are parked at the Blue Lagoon use the path described at the end of Walk No.1.1 to reach the top of Winter Hill but bear left to find the tarmac road as soon as you see it.

Continue along the tarmac to the T.V. station. If you want the quickest route to the Pike - and be warned, it is exceedingly boggy -

turn right at the T.V. station and pick up a track made of railway sleepers at the end of their car park. The sleepers don't last long and you will flounder in bog before you reach the little bridge across the infant River Douglas. The Pike lies straight ahead.

If dry feet seem attractive so early in a long day, stay on the tarmac until it starts to make a big curve to the left. On your right a grassy track marked by a small cairn cuts down the moor to Pike Cottage whence a right turn and 10 minutes sees you on the Pike.

Now follow the previous walk until you reach Holcombe Tower and from there get to Jumbles Reservoir by following the appropriate section of the next walk, Spanner's Round.

At Jumbles Reservoir car park keep straight ahead past the Information Centre caravan along the reservoir banks. Cross the bridge, go up the steps through the wood and into the pastures where the track continues to the road. Turn right and at the road junction in Chapeltown turn left into a cindery lane. Turn left where it meets another lane near a mill and continue to the fields. Keep straight ahead up a cart track which becomes a footpath, through the wood onto the brow of the hill. Here a well-trodden track turns right to the top of Chetham Close but you keep straight on at the stile.

Soon you will drop down to a long wall close to the shale spoil heaps of some long disused colliery. Go through the stile and turn right. The path follows the wall for a time then bears left down the hill to join a wide grassy track. Turn right here and go back up the hill to a wall corner. (This manoeuvre keeps you on right of way tracks.) The wall corner can be a bit confusing, there are two stiles and you want the upper and not very obvious one. Now follow the clear path through the pastures to Horrobins, just visible behind the trees. There are good views across Dimple Reservoir to Winter Hill from this track, whilst Belmont, your ultimate goal, has come into sight but may be difficult to see against a late sun. You will reach the grassy cart track leading to Horrobins before you reach the buildings. Turn left on it and follow it down past 'The Highlands'. As its access road starts to curve right, look on the left for a stile. There's no path to start with, but bear well to the left aiming at the house with the white gable end to find the stile. Turn right on this road and continue to the main road in Egerton.

Go straight across the road and follow the grassy lane behind the pub to a T-junction. Turn left and follow a wet cart track past the first piece of woodland. The cart track becomes much better and turns left at the second piece of woodland. You, however, keep straight on (the path is signed) across the stream and through more woodland. When you emerge follow the path down to the next stream then the side of the wood to the road. Turn left here and keep going to Belmont, a good mile away. When you reach the main road turn right to find the 'Dog' and left there to find the Blue Lagoon.

SHERBORNE'S SAUNTER   WALK NO.5.2

Named in memory of Bill Sherborne, a Bolton man who knew these moors better than most. It links together the best of a number of walks already given in this book to make a whole day's walk, taking 7-8 hours. Though not as long as Spanner's Way it is more demanding because of the greater height made.

Rivington to White Coppice
Park at the Hall Barn and leave the car park by the rough road to Rivington village that leaves the car park close to its entrance. From Rivington village follow Walk No.1.8 and its extension to the path along the Anglezarke Reservoir just below the High Bullough Reservoir. Turn right here and follow this 'restored' path to the road at the Waterman's Cottage. Cross the road and go through the swing gate, then turn left. Follow the wettish footpath and where it is about to cross a bridge over the Goit, keep straight on along a rough stony cart track. Follow it all the way to White Coppice.

White Coppice to Darwen Tower
Keep straight on at the next bridge over the Goit then make a sharp turn right (Walk No.1.12) to climb up the wide track up the escarpment. Continue to follow the well-trodden track all the way up Great Hill. Here you have a clear view of your next objective, Darwen Tower, as well as the Lake District hills on a good day. Keep straight on at the large cairn on top, but when you have gone down the steep bit, and gained the wet moor bear right a little away from the trees on your left. The track will take you down to the stream which is out of sight. Cross it and keep straight on to the isolated building on the road ahead. Cross the road, turn right on it and left through a swing gate after about 100 yards. Continue along the cart track until it bends sharply right. Here you take a branch on the left, but first it is worth your while bearing right to have a look at the Wishing Well of Hollinshead Hall. See Walk No.4.8 for information about it. In any case it offers shelter for lunch should the day be a poor one. Back to that left-hand branch. Follow it for about 100 yards when you will see the

177

junction leading to the Slipper Lowe car park on the right. Turn into it and from here follow the route to Darwen Tower, Walk No.4.4.

Darwen Tower to Belmont

From Darwen Tower, an excellent viewpoint of all things north-west to north-east on a clear day, turn right following the path along the edge of the moor for a considerable distance. Paths join it from both sides, you just keep straight on above the wall/fence until you come to Duckshaw Clough. As you drop into this deep cut rocky defile look out for a grassy cart track on your right leading to old quarry workings. If you miss it, no matter, you merely go down to the tarmac road in the defile, turn right and make up the height you have lost. Follow this track up onto the moor, take the left-hand branch and follow its very agreeable wanderings over the moor until it joins the Belmont-Turton track - agreeable that is to say except the last few hundred yards which are very wet. Turn right on the Belmont track and follow it to the wall - there's some shelter for a bite to eat here, then continue down the well-marked track over a stile then through a wide gap in the wall onto a cindery cart track. Here turn left and follow it through a derelict farmyard to Pasture Barn Farm. Turn right through the farm then left and follow its access road to the dam of the Belmont Reservoir. Turn right here and left when you reach the main road.

Belmont to Rivington

Here you are on the fringe of the village which will offer you some refreshment if your timing is right. Walking down the hill the village shop is on your left and open on Sundays until 5.00 p.m. The Black Bull is almost opposite and keeps pub hours. You need go no further, for you turn right into the street just above the pub. New stone-built flats or town houses now occupy the site marked with a church on the 1:25,000 map and help to identify which of the many side streets you need. After you have passed the last house on the left which bears a plaque 'Bethel Chapel built 1838' turn left down the side of the wall and follow the little track round the side of the playing fields onto the road. Go straight across and follow the footpath round the other side and up the banks of the inlet stream until you are below a car parking area. From it a well-trodden track leads to the summit of Winter Hill. You may prefer to backtrack a little and follow the road round to the TV mast as it is very rough going to cut across, if shorter. From the private car park at the mast a little track runs left in the direction of the Pike. It quickly becomes a wide boggy swathe, exceedingly wet,

178

but it leads direct to the Pike. From the top of the Pike, a superb viewpoint late in the day with the sun low in the western sky, make for the near corner of the Terrace Gardens below on the right. From here the most direct route to the Hall Barn is to stay on this top terrace until you come to the pond almost at the Pigeon Tower. Here go down the great flight of steps, designed by Leverhulme himself, right to their end. Then a choice of variously steep and direct tracks takes you into the lower point of the woods and straight down the field to the rough road above the Hall Barn. Go straight across and into the lower woods bearing right to get back to the Hall Barn.

Shortest Route from Belmont to the Hall Barn

Should you, for any reason, wish to curtail the route, at least 30 minutes and much energy can be saved by using the following route from Belmont: When you have passed the former Bethel Chapel keep straight on over the stile. At the site of the former farm ahead cross another stile, turn left and follow the well-marked if wet track right up to the top of the road. Here follow the road for a good half mile to where it makes a sharp right-hand bend. On the left there is a newish stile, cross this, go down the hill to find another stile and an obvious line of stiles and bridges puts you in a vast green pasture. Now simply follow the fence, walking on springy green turf until you reach the car parking area at Old Kate's Dingle. Go straight across to another stile, straight on to the next, then follow the fence round to yet another one. Over this turn left and immediately left again onto a cinder cart track. Take the right-hand fork within a few yards and 7 or 8 minutes will see you in the Hall Barn car park.

SPANNER'S ROUND   WALK NO.5.3

This walk, a 20 miler, was devised by Derek Magnall, secretary of the East Lancashire Section of the Long Distance Walkers' Association and named, it is said, after his dog, Spanner. It is a very fine circular walk, one of the best in the whole book if you are in the 20 mile a day class. If not, it can be split into two parts of not quite equal length at Calf Hey Reservoir.

The Preliminaries

The walk starts at Jumbles Reservoir car park but it could be started equally well from Clough Head car park at Haslingden Grane, though that start would lack the slow unfolding of the scene which is one of the attractions of the Jumbles start. Jumbles can be reached using the Bolton to Burnley bus, No.273. People living in Blackburn and using public transport could start from Bromley Cross station, though this would add a couple of miles to the day and the anxiety of getting a train back home. On the other hand Blackburn people who want to do the walk in two halves are well placed, for they could finish at Calf Hey Reservoir, though the bus service, Blackburn-Rochdale, is only a two hourly one. If you are not sure whether you are in the 20 mile a day class and cannot arrange to be met on request, then bear three things in mind:

1. The first place from which you can get a direct bus back to Jumbles if you are too late or too tired to finish is Ramsbottom, which is on the No.273 route. It runs hourly at 6 minutes past the hour (in 1986, so check before you start) even on Sundays, from the Market Place in Ramsbottom. This would save you a couple of hours. You can pick up the same bus at Holcombe Brook or at Hawkeshaw, but by then you are almost home.

2. The walk as described contains an almost closed loop to Turton and Entwistle Reservoir that probably adds on about a mile and can be omitted without loss of character.

3. Route finding from Wayoh Fold Farm to Great House Farm, Musbury is often quite difficult and can be time consuming.

One final point. The route goes through the Army firing range at Holcombe. Check that the red flags are not flying. See Walk No.3.1.

The Route to Wayoh Fold Farm

Leave the car park passing the Information Caravan and follow the wide gravel track along the reservoir bank. Keep straight ahead at the bridge and follow the footpath up the stream to Turton Bottoms. The path divides several times, just keep near the brook and you will come out in a former works yard in the Bottoms. Turn left across the bridge and continue to the road. Turn right here and walk up the hill for 7 or 8 minutes to the Black Bull then go down the path immediately beyond it. It will lead you onto the embankment of the Wayoh Reservoir but you barely reach it before you are directed by a path diversion to climb the bank on your right and follow the path through the fields. Follow it over the hill and come right down again to water level. Then follow the well-marked path to the road. Go straight across and continue the length of the reservoir crossing two inlet streams by good wooden bridges.

The Loop to Turton and Entwistle Reservoir

After the second bridge leave the track that encircles the reservoir and climb up a wide grassy cart track through the wood into a couple of fields onto the road just below the Strawberry Duck and Entwistle Station. Turn right, go left in front of the pub and continue along a wide cinder track to the road at the reservoir embankment. Turn right here and continue along it to a narrow fenced path through the wood on the right. It is not obvious but it will only take you about five minutes. When you reach the lane turn right and in about 100 yards turn left onto the access road leading to Broadmeadow Farm and Stables. At the end of the buildings on the left of the farm road look for a signposted footpath. Follow the path downhill, go under the railway and drop down to the small reservoir above Wayoh Reservoir, easily seen well to the right. You will see a stile and bridge below you on your left. Here you rejoin the main route.

The Main Route, continued

If you are omitting the loop bear right as soon as you have located the grassy cart track to find a stile and keep on this line to find the stile and bridge mentioned above. Follow the clear track up to Wayoh Fold Farm, passing to the left of the buildings and continue to the road. It follows the course of the Roman road that ran from Manchester, or some do say from Wigan, to Blackburn and Ribchester.

From Wayoh Fold Farm to Calf Hey Reservoir

Turn left on the road and in about 100 yards turn right along a signed cart track. At the fork take the lower one and follow it to the disused Lower House Farm. Pass the farm on its right (It can be extremely muddy) and turn left at the end of its buildings. Then go through the iron gate straight ahead and in the field bear diagonally right across a big patch of rushes to find the path leading to a gap in the wall.

Continue in the same direction following the fence down to the stream and then go past Longshoot Farm by a diverted path on its left. Turn right before the second stile and passing a wooden cabin leave that field to reach the farm access road. Turn left and follow it until it starts to bear left in front of a wood. Here look for a little path that runs to the nearby fence. Follow it up the fence, go through a decrepit stile close to a gate and continue following the fence, to the end of the wood. Cross the wire (there's no stile) into the field, turn left and follow the faint path close to the line of the wood up to the road.

Go straight across the road and up the lane to the farm passing it on its left. Continue on faint paths to the top of Hog Lowe Pike, a very

181

fine viewpoint on a good day. Pendle Hill lies ahead, Boulsworth to its right, Cribden (which overlooks Haslingden) is in front of Boulsworth and the flat top of Whitworth Moor is prominent to its right. Behind you the TV masts on Winter Hill are clear to see, so too, is Darwen Tower perched on the end of the moor. Leave the Pike by the path to the right and as soon as you have crossed the stile bear left down the little valley. Cross another stile and then go right across the valley itself. The path now becomes clearer and gradually drops down the flank of the valley passing below a boulder on which the letters SP (Spanner?) are painted. You come down to the fence and eventually a stile takes you out of the valley onto a narrow path that travels along the hillside with good views of Calf Hey Reservoir.

Exit to Clough Head Car Park (about 15 minutes)

If you are leaving the route take note when you are approaching the end of the reservoir and look for a stile near a large solitary tree. Cross the embankment here and a few minutes sees you in Calf Hey car park and a few more across the road in Clough Head car park.

From Calf Hey Reservoir to Holcombe Tower

Continuing from the stile, at the first stream after passing a ruined farm the path forks. Take the upper one and climb quite steeply up the hillside into the old quarry on Musbury Heights. You will see the stump of an old chimney on the right. Turn left and follow the twists and turns of a wide grassy track amongst the old quarry workings until you come to a gap in the wall and emerge into the Musbury Valley by a waymarker post.

The way lies straight ahead though the path is faint at first. From this point you can see it clearly across the far side of the valley for it contours round the head at this level. First drop down a little to two trees then follow a raised bank until you are within sight of one of the many ruined farms. Then make towards it. Leave it by a gateway on the left and follow a well-trodden path through a gateway. Cross a stream and climb up to a bigger track. Now follow this right round the head of the valley crossing two streams. Then climb up gently to the right following the path to a stile into a green field, a great contrast with the rest of the rough grasses of the moor.

Follow the track down to the gate leading to Great House Farm and go over the stile besides it. Drop down onto a concrete cart track and follow it up the valley. It ends at the third barn, but a good grass track continues round the head of the valley crossing two streams and then climbs up the other side. At the wall corner take the upper track, the lower cart track soon dwindles to a footpath and then disappears. By this time you are within sight of the red painted notice boards warning you to keep out if the red flags are flying. Make for the notice board and you will pick up a well-trodden footpath leading to the site of the Pilgrim's Cross. Continue past the site following the path to Holcombe Hill and Peel's Monument.

Exit to Ramsbottom (about 20 minutes)
In the last dip before Holcombe Hill, easily identified by the old quarry to the left, you will find a footpath leading to Harcles Hill Farm. When you reach the rough lane below this farm go straight across it and through the wicker gate into a narrow walled lane. Follow this to the tarmac and again go straight across over a stile onto a footpath fenced with barbed wire. Some 50 yards down leave it by a stile on the left. Now follow a narrow but well-trodden path down a little valley bearing right then left to reach a rough lane leading to the road. Five minutes down this sees you to the main Burnley road and the bus stop.

Holcombe Hill to Hawkeshaw
At the Monument, a very good viewpoint over south Lancashire on a good day, take the path signposed to Holcombe Village. Turn right over a stile at the end of the wall and follow the fence down. Where it and the main track turn sharp left take the minor track to the right. It will bring you at once onto Moorbottom Lane. Go straight across it into the field, go straight down it and the next one to reach a stile by another War Office notice. Continue straight down the fence and at the stile into the wood bear right and follow the fence down to the stream. Cross it easily, turn left and follow this second bigger stream for a little way, then leave it and climb up towards Redisher Farm. Turn right as soon as you are over the stile and turn right again in a few yards along a wide cinder track to Hollingrove Farm. At the farm take the diversionary track to the left, turn left on the track leading to the farm and follow it to the next house. Turn left into the field just beyond it and continue to the brook. Now turn left and follow the brook to the next stile then keep going in this direction until you reach a farm access road. Go straight across through the swing gate and keep going until you reach Hawkeshaw opposite the mill marked on the map SD 61/71. If you are on your last legs you can get the bus from Hawkeshaw back to Jumbles.

Hawkeshaw to Jumbles

Cross the road and turn right then turn left down the first wide lane barely 100 yards away. It ends at a cottage, Sunny Top, but a path continues from the corner on the right going down the field. As you approach the stream turn right over a ladder stile then left through the gate and make towards the farm. You should find yellow waymarkers, but they have nothing to do with Spanner's Round. However, follow them to the stile above the farm, then climb steeply up the hill. Pass between two small reservoirs and keep straight ahead to reach the Tottington road. Cross the road and turn right. Almost at once turn left into a farm access road, but by pass the farm on its left just before you reach it. This path, fenced at first then walled will bring you to Affetside at the side of the Pack Horse.

Cross the road and turn right down a short lane between the bungalow and the bus turning circle. (The cross is but a few yards further on. See page 27 for information.) The lane leads you into the fields and the way on lies straight down the hill following tractor marks. Given a clear evening, there are very fine views indeed of Helsby, Frodsham and the Welsh Hills. At the iron fence of the water works enclosure turn left and join its access road to reach the main road. Go straight across this into the lane and follow it up the last little hill into the car park.

MEDIUM DISTANCE FOOTPATHS
GOING THROUGH THE AREA

1. The Douglas Way

The Douglas Way is a middle distance footpath of some 36 miles following the length of the Douglas valley from its source on Winter Hill to the Ribble Estuary. Necessarily its passage through the West Pennine Moors is brief. The work has been done by the Bolton Rambler's Association but as yet the guide book has not been published.

2. The Lancashire Trail

This long distance route was devised by the St. Helens and District C.H.A. and H.F. Rambling Club to commemorate their Golden Jubilee. The route starts, naturally, in St. Helens and finishes at Thornton in Craven. It enters the West Pennine Moors Recreation Area at Horwich, and leaves it at Abbey Village having gone through Lever Park, along the reservoirs, over Great Hill and along the River Roddlesworth; all walks covered by this guide. The guide to it was published by the St. Helens and District C.H.A. and H.F. Rambling Club.

3. The Rossendale Way

The Rossendale Way is a 45 mile circuit of the Borough of Rossendale using the moorland fringes as far as practicable. About a third of it lies within the Area, from just north of Haslingden to Stubbins. It is the brain-child of Ian Goldthorpe who devised the route, did the research for the extensive background information it contains and wrote the guidebook. It is published by Rossendale Groundwork Trust Ltd.

4. Trans-Pennine Walk

This is a 54 mile route from Adlington to Haworth. It has been worked out and the guidebook written by Richard Mackrory, published by the Dalesman Press, 1983. The walk uses field paths and roads to get to Rivington, then follows the route of the Three Towers Walk - though not in every detail - as far as Lower Grainings Farm. From here it takes a low level route to Holcombe Brook and there leaves the West Pennine Moors Recreation Area.

CICERONE PRESS
WALKING GUIDES - U.K.

THE RIBBLE WAY
Gladys Sellers
The long distance path from sea to source.

WHITE PEAK WALKS
The Northern Dales
WHITE PEAK WALKS
The Southern Dales
HIGH PEAK WALKS
Mark Richards
Three books which cover the whole of the Peak District. Illustrated in Mark's distinctive style with beautiful drawings and maps.

THE YORKSHIRE DALES
A Guide to the National Park
Gladys Sellers
A comprehensive, practical guide to the best walking in the Dales.

WALKING ON DARTMOOR
John Earle
A comprehensive guide to the National Park.

WALKING ON THE NORTH YORK MOORS
Martin Collins
A practical guide to the best this area has to offer.

WALKS IN THE ARNSIDE/SILVERDALE AREA *Brian Evans*
A well illustrated companion guide to this compact yet delectable area.

THE ISLE OF MAN COASTAL PATH
Aileen Evans
A guide to this lovely unspoilt coastline path and other LD walks.

WALKING GUIDES - EUROPE

WALKING IN MALLORCA
June Parker

MOUNTAIN WALKING IN AUSTRIA *Cecil Davies*

WALKS & CLIMBS IN THE PYRENEES *Kev Reynolds*

WALKS IN THE ENGADINE, SWITZERLAND *Martin Collins*

CHAMONIX-MONT-BLANC
A Walking Guide
Martin Collins

TOUR OF MONT BLANC
Andrew Harper

WALKS IN THE VALAIS -SWITZERLAND *Kev Reynolds*

ALTA VIA - DOLOMITE HIGH LEVEL ROUTE
Martin Collins

These are just some of the guide books which Cicerone Press produce. Send for catalogue of the full range of walking, climbing, scrambling and outdoor books.
Available from bookshops, outdoor equipment shops or direct from:
CICERONE PRESS, 2 Police Square, Milnthorpe, Cumbria LA7 7PY

Printed by Carnmor Print & Design,
95/97, London Road, Preston, Lancashire.